The Guide to Caring for Bi-racial or African American Children's Natural Hair

By Krika Bradsher

Table of Contents

Section IV Styling Guide

Section I
An Introduction to Caring for Curly and Kinky Natural Hair

Chapter One
Learning to Care for Biracial and African American Hair

As a stylist who specializes in helping my clients establish and maintain healthy, natural hair, I've encountered many mothers of biracial and African American children who are struggling to care for their children's hair. They're frustrated because they love their children and want to give them the very best of everything, including hair care. Yet, they've found this seemingly simple task more complicated than they imagined. Why?

Because their children's hair is nothing like theirs.

The difference may not have seemed significant in the beginning. However, a few months, or years, of struggling with their children's hair has proved otherwise. Recognizing that your child's hair is very different from yours is just the beginning. Knowing *how* to care for your child's hair is another matter altogether.

If you are lucky enough to have a diverse support network of family, friends, neighbors and co-workers, they can be an invaluable source for advice on caring for black and biracial hair. Unfortunately, not everyone has this luxury, and those who do may be reluctant to request help.

Why?

One mother revealed that she was ashamed to go to her friends and co-workers to ask for advice about how to care for her African American daughter's hair. Doing so made her feel like a failure as a mother. She felt that she should be able to care for her daughter's hair on her own.

I understand this mother's frustration. Caring for your child's hair may seem like a basic element of motherhood. However, life is rarely that simple.

This brings us to two critical points that I need to make crystal clear before we go any further.

#1: Not knowing how to care for your biracial or African American child's hair *does not make you an inadequate parent.*

It simply means that you are unfamiliar with a hair type that may differ greatly from your own. The fact that you've picked up this book and are actively seeking advice on how to care for your child's hair demonstrates your commitment to your child's well-being. I applaud you for recognizing that your child's hair requires something more and for making the effort to learn what you should be doing instead. That brings me to the next point, perhaps the most important lesson of this entire book.

#2: It's okay to ask for help.

Professional stylists, friends and family *want* to help you in your quest to make your son or daughter's hair look its very best. So don't be afraid to seek help, whether in the pages of a book, at a local salon specializing in natural hair care, or at your child's playgroup.

If you are a Caucasian parent, agonizing over how to care for your African American or biracial child's hair, I'll tell you a little secret. **Many biracial and African American men and women struggle with the best way to care for their hair or their children's hair, too.**

Just as your hair may be very different (in color, texture or the way it behaves) from that of your siblings or parents, people with curly, kinky and wavy hair often have very different hair from their parents and siblings, too. Because of this, many of us have discovered what works best through trial and error. The knowledge and expertise we currently possess is the result of experimentation <u>and lots of bad hair days</u>.

We've established that you shouldn't feel guilty about not instinctively knowing how to care for your child's hair, but let's be clear about another point:

Not knowing how to care for your child's hair doesn't give you a free pass to let your child's hair look like who done it and why.

Think of it as driving a car in an unfamiliar town. Perhaps you are unaware of all of the traffic laws. For instance, North Carolinians might be surprised to discover that the U-turns we make so routinely here will earn them a moving violation and a hefty fine in Ohio. Sure, it's an honest mistake. Yet, this doesn't protect the driver from the consequences of actions committed in ignorance.

We'll discuss the many reasons it's essential to make your child's hair look its best, later in this section. But for now, let's examine the physical characteristics that make biracial and African American hair unique.

Chapter Two
The Physical Differences Between Caucasian Hair & Biracial and African American Hair

We've established that there's a difference between Caucasian hair and biracial or African American hair. Now let's explore the physical characteristics that create this difference, so that you'll better understand your child's hair.

Once you get a clearer understanding of the properties of textured hair, your son or daughter's hair will become less of a mystery. Right now, you're probably frustrated because—whether it's wavy, curly or tightly coiled—your child's hair has been problematic for both of you. This book is designed not only to help resolve this issue, but to change the narrative you and your child have created about his or her hair.

Our hair is an important part of our identity. Viewing such a key component of one's identity as problematic can create serious self-esteem issues for your child. We'll talk more about this in a bit. For now, remember that your attitude about your child's hair (how you refer to it, facial expressions related to your child's hair care, and how you treat your child's hair) will have a major impact on how the child views herself.

Don't speak negatively about your child's hair, and encourage her not to either.

As we review the ways your child's hair may be different from yours, think of it as just that—different. Not bad, ugly or undesirable, just different. Perhaps even unique.

Textured Hair is Fragile

You probably weren't expecting to hear that. In fact, many mistakenly believe that textured hair is stronger than Caucasian hair.

That misconception is held across ethnicities. Textured hair looks thicker. Therefore, we assume it is stronger and more durable than Caucasian or Asian hair.

It isn't.

Compare a strand of textured hair with your own. You'll notice that there are bends and twists in the strand. At the points where the strand changes direction, it is often thinner and weaker. In fact, the width of the strand isn't consistent from root to tip. This makes the hair more vulnerable to breakage. Also, if you looked at the strands under a microscope, the textured hair would appear flattened, or elliptical in shape, rather than round, as Caucasian hair strands tend to be. Textured strands also tend not to grow in as densely as straighter hair typically does.

Grasp one naturally shed strand of your hair between the thumb and forefinger of each hand. Give it a tug until you exert enough force to make it snap. Now do the same with a naturally shed strand of your child's hair. It will likely take a lot less force for the textured strand to snap. Since your child's hair is more fragile, it must be handled more delicately.

We'll go into more details about how to care for your child's hair in Section Three of this book. However, keep the fragility of your child's hair in mind when caring for it. For instance, avoid small tooth combs, brushes with bristles that will tear at the hair and hair accessories that tug and pull at the hair.

Textured Hair Tangles More Easily

The bends and twists in the strand contribute to textured hair becoming tangled easily. Those hooks and bends get enmeshed. The longer textured hair goes without being combed and detangled, the more matted it gets.

Combing and detangling your child's hair can be traumatic for both of you, especially when done incorrectly. Periodically I'll consult with a client who has essentially given up combing her child's hair because it's become a nightmare for the entire family. The child's hair will be badly matted and damaged because it hasn't been detangled regularly. So let's take a moment to address another important issue:

Detangling your child's hair is <u>not</u> optional.

Children go through periods when they don't want to brush their teeth or take a bath. As their parents, we insist that they do. *Grooming your child's hair is no different.* That being said, learning how to properly comb and detangle the child's hair will make the process easier for both of you.

Handle your child's hair gently when combing. Detangle, preferably when damp and while being conditioned. Start at the ends of the hair— the most fragile part of the strand. Hold onto the section being combed, just above where you're combing or detangling the hair. Slowly move up the strand until the entire section is finished. Twist gently so that the detangled hair does tangle back up with loose strands. Go on to the next section.

Biracial and African American Tresses are Drier

Another notable difference in textured hair is that it tends to be drier. Remember how the strand of your child's hair you examined had bends and kinks in it? The structure of the hair fiber also plays a role in the dryness of textured hair.

Your scalp produces oil. In straight hair, that oil makes its way down the hair shaft. Consequently, straight hair that hasn't been washed for several days tends to look weighed down and greasy. However, natural scalp oils find it more difficult to travel the windy path of textured hair.

As a result, textured hair—especially the ends—gets dry and brittle. Since the natural oils aren't able to moisturize the hair shaft, we must.

Daily moisture is _essential_ for healthy biracial and African American hair.

This is one of the most important lessons to understand about your child's hair. It needs moisture. Since the scalp isn't able to provide it on its own, you must moisturize your child's hair regularly to keep it healthy and vibrant. Dry hair gets brittle and breaks more easily, especially when manipulated.

We'll discuss products and methods you can use to keep your child's hair moisturized in a later section of the book. However, nothing is more hydrating to your child's hair than water. Don't be afraid to wet your child's hair, especially before combing or manipulation. Apply a heavier product, like moisturizer, oil or hair butter, after spraying the hair with water, in order to retain moisture.

The importance of moisture to textured hair is something that many have only come to understand in the last decade, thanks in large part to the natural hair movement. In fact, many women of color still believe water isn't good for their hair. Be aware of this, in case some well-meaning soul advises you against wetting your child's hair frequently.

The elasticity, or springiness, of textured hair is predicated upon moisture. Biracial and African American hair tends to have more elasticity than Caucasian hair. This ability to bounce back helps protect the hair from breakage during combing, braiding and other types of manipulation. Dry hair loses its elasticity and snaps off under stress, rather than bouncing back to its original state. Without elasticity, your child's hair is more susceptible to breakage. So when it comes to your child's hair: moisturize, moisturize, moisturize!

Fight the Frizz

You may have noticed that biracial and African American hair tends to get frizzy under certain conditions. To understand why this happens, let's quickly visualize the structure of the cuticle. The cuticle is the protective outer layer of each hair strand. It is often described as being similar to a roof with overlapping shingles. The shingles represent the overlapping protein layers which form the cuticle. When the cuticle is smooth, or undamaged, those shingles lie flat. When the cuticle is damaged (by chemical treatments, environmental damage, brushing of dry hair, etc), the shingles lift.

Dry, thirsty hair becomes frizzy when it encounters humidity. The hair draws moisture from the air, lifting those "shingles" and causing each strand to puff up. Frizz can't always be eliminated completely. However, hair that has been moisturized and sealed, by applying a natural oil or hair butter, is less likely to become frizzy in response to humidity. Protective styles, which we'll discuss later, are also a good way to combat frizz in humid situations.

Textured Hair Isn't as Shiny

The structure of biracial and African American hair, with its endless twists and curves, contributes to another difference. Even when your child's hair is healthy and moisturized, it won't look as shiny as healthy, straight hair does. That's because straight hair reflects light, making it look glossy. The textured pattern of your child's hair handles light differently. Since it doesn't have the same straight, smooth surface, it doesn't reflect light the same way. Healthy, textured hair has sheen, rather than a glossy shine. So it may look dull when compared with straight hair. This is natural. As long as your child's hair is healthy and moisturized, it's fine.

The "Tender-Headed" Syndrome

Remember those parents who'd given up on combing and detangling their children's hair? Each parent started out determined to properly care for his or her child's hair. However, the experience was upsetting for everyone, *especially the child*. Many children are what we refer to as "tender-headed." In other words, they find it painful, even torturous, to have their hair combed or braided. If this has been your experience, take heart. Grooming your child's hair can be a pleasant experience for both of you—once you know how.

First, having a "tender head" or sensitive scalp isn't something that only children experience. Many adults still complain of being "tender-headed." There are three types of "tender heads." Some children and adults have more sensitive scalps. It's simply part of their nature. For others, there could be an underlying condition, such as psoriasis or an allergic reaction to harsh, drying shampoos or hair products containing caustic chemicals (like relaxers). However, the majority of clients I've serviced with tender heads had trauma inflicted on the scalp due to improper grooming and styling techniques. Some of the biggest culprits are:

- Aggressive combing and brushing;
- Ponytails and braids that are far too tight; and
- Using the wrong styling tools (like small tooth combs and brushes with hard, unforgiving bristles).

The tools and techniques referenced above yank the hair, causing scalp soreness. The more frequently this is done, the more sensitive the child's scalp becomes. Add to this the fear and anxiety the child feels in anticipation of traumatic grooming sessions. Is it any wonder some children are terrified of having their hair combed or braided?

In Section Three, we'll cover step-by-step techniques to properly care for your child's hair. However, here are two important concepts to understand about tender-headedness:

1. <u>Patience is a virtue.</u>

2. **Your child will internalize the verbal *and non-verbal* messages you create about his or her hair.**

Patience is a must when grooming textured hair. It's a process that must be repeated frequently. Why not make it as enjoyable as possible for you and your child?

Here are a few tips that will improve your child's hair care experience:

1. Schedule adequate time to groom your child's hair, so neither of you feels rushed or stressed.

2. Create a fun, relaxing hair care routine. Perhaps incorporate an educational show, an audiobook, or allow your child to play with a special "hair time" toy during grooming.

3. Create positive messages surrounding your child's hair. Saying "It's time to make your hair pretty for school" will boost the child's self-esteem. Sighing and groaning, "I have to do something with your head" makes the child feel like her hair is a problem that must be solved. (More on this in a later chapter.)

4. Remember, it's not only the words used when speaking about your child's hair. Only seven percent of our message is conveyed through the words we use. The majority of the message is derived from body language and facial expressions.

Incorporate some of the tips above in your child's hair care routine. Finding time to create a peaceful hair care routine can be challenging with our already hectic schedules. Yet, the benefits are well worth it for you and your child.

Obviously, if there is a medical condition causing your child's sensitive scalp, you'll need to seek the help of a dermatologist. However, even in cases when your child's scalp in naturally sensitive, or there is a medical issue present, applying the techniques listed above will still help alleviate the situation.

Now that you understand the physical attributes of your child's hair, it's time to assess your child's hair type. We'll explore the various textured hair types and discuss why it's important to understand each child's particular hair type.

Chapter Three
How to Determine Your Child's Hair Type and Why It Matters

As noted before, biracial and African American hair comes in a variety of textures that include waves, curls and coils. There is a growing call to stop using hair types, as some worry that it creates divisions within the natural hair community. However, as you learn to care for your child's hair, it's useful to have a thorough understanding of the basic textured hair types, since each has distinct characteristics and reacts differently to hair products, treatments and styling methods. Let's take a moment to briefly review each hair texture type.

Type 1 – Straight

Though we're discussing textured hair, let's start with Type I, straight hair, so that we have a good comparison of the characteristics that make African American and biracial hair quite different from straight hair. This category includes hair that is naturally straight as well as hair that has been chemically-straightened. Within this type there are three subcategories (as there are within each hair type).

In straight hair that is fine and thin (1A) the cuticles lay flat, so the hair easily reflects light and tends to look shiny and "healthy." Because the hair shaft is bone straight, oil from the scalp easily travel to the ends of the hair. Therefore, 1A hair requires frequent washing to prevent hair from looking oily. This hair type doesn't easily hold a curl.

Straight, medium hair (1B) strands are a bit thicker. This hair type tends to have more volume and body. This makes it easier for the hair to hold a curl. On the other hand, straight, coarse hair (1C) is bone-straight; yet it is resistant to holding a curl.

Type 2 – Wavy Hair

This is where we begin to see texture in the hair. Rather than being completely straight, there is a slight curve pattern than can range from barely-there waves that lie close to the head and have lots of sheen (2A) to a more defined, but gentle wave (2B) and then finally, a well-defined, but extremely loose curl pattern (2C). Type 2 hair is often wavy at the roots, but tends to be curlier at the ends. While Type 2A hair can be styled fairly easily. Types 2B and 2C are more resistant to styling and tend to frizz.

Type 3 – Curly Hair

We'll spend most of our time in this section describing Type 3 and Type 4 hair since the majority of African American and biracial hair falls within these categories.

Type 3A hair typically consists of big, loose, springy, S-shaped curls. The curls often have some gloss to them. The hair tends to become a bit frizzy when subjected to humidity.

Type 3B hair has lots of well-defined spirals that can range from soft, bouncy ringlets to tighter, corkscrew curls. The strands are often coarser than 3A strands and the tighter spiral also lessens the shine of 3B hair. This hair type also tends to get frizzy in humid weather.

Type 3C hair typically consists of tight, corkscrew curls that can sometimes be kinky in texture. In people with this hair type, the strands of hair grow denser, giving the hair more volume. Though the hair is dense and voluminous, individual strands may be fine in texture.

When wet, Type 3 hair looks straighter and stretches out closer to its full length. As the hair dries, the curls tighten. Strands shrink to a fraction of their full length. This is called "shrinkage" and is typical in Type 3 and Type 4 hair.

Type 4 – Kinky and Coily

Type 4 hair can be fine and thin or wiry and coarse. This hair type tends to have more densely packed strands. While Type 4 hair looks thicker and perhaps tougher than the other types of hair, this is deceptive. Type 4 hair doesn't have as many cuticle layers as Type 1 or 2 hair, so it's actually weaker and more fragile. This makes the hair quite susceptible to breakage caused by daily styling routines. Unfortunately, Type 4 hair is frequently subjected to the most abuse in an effort to make the hair look straighter and more "manageable."

Type 4A hair has a tightly coiled S-pattern (though you may need to stretch the hair slightly to see it). Type 4B has more of a Z-pattern. This hair type also tends to be wiry. Type 4C has a zigzag pattern, similar to that of Type 4B. However, the tight, kinky pattern causes the hair to appear to have very little curl definition, if any. Another important difference in Type 4 hair: even when it's healthy, it won't have the glossy shine found in less coily hair types. In comparison, healthy Type 4 hair, which has a low sheen, may appear dull.

Moisture is essential to all hair types. However, for Type 4 hair, daily moisture is *critical* to the health of the hair. Already fragile, when Type 4 hair becomes dry and brittle it is even more susceptible to damage and breakage.

Now that you understand the hair types, how can you determine your child's hair type and why is it important to know?

Determining Your Child's Hair Type

To determine your child's natural hair type, you'll need to see the hair in its natural state. Wash your child's hair so that it is free of any products. Then allow it to dry naturally. Carefully examine the hair pattern and texture, comparing it to the chart listed below:

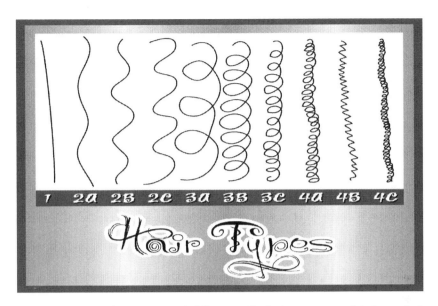

Now that you know your child's specific hair type, use this knowledge to make healthier product, treatment and hairstyling choices for your child's hair. Keep your child's type in mind as we discuss various hair products and styling methods. But first, there are three points I need to make clear regarding hair types.

Three Critical Points to Understand About Hair Types

There is no "good" or "bad" hair. There are just various types of hair, each with its own beauty and challenges.

Earlier I mentioned that many in the natural hair community find hair typing to be divisive. Here's why: Straight and wavy hair is often categorized as "good hair" while tightly curled or coily hair is judged harshly. If you use terms like "nappy" to describe your child's 4C hair, you're sending the message that her hair is *difficult, inferior* or even *ugly*. Comments like, "Wow your hair is nappy today," might *seem* innocent. However, such statements form the foundation of the narrative your child will develop about her hair. This can lead to a poor self-image and a negative relationship with her hair that can have a lifelong effect.

It is common for one person to have multiple hair types.

This is a reality that many naturals find it tough to come to terms with. Frequently, we have more than one hair type. For instance, the hair at the front on one side of the head might be 3C. Perhaps the hair at the crown of the head is 4B while hair at the nape of the neck (frequently called "the kitchen") is 4A.

This makes it more challenging to get a consistent, unified look throughout the head. However, once you understand the various types, tweaks and adjustments can make the differences less noticeable. Another option is to enlist a stylist experienced with natural hair to cut and style the child's hair in a way that acknowledges the different hair types and blends them harmoniously.

No two heads of hair are exactly alike—even if they share hair types.

Don't beat yourself up if you can't get your child's hair to look like the video blogger whose hair is the same type as your child's. Hair of the same type shares many characteristics. That's why people with 4C hair are more likely to find success using similar products. However, your child's hair is unique. Don't be surprised if a particular brand or a certain kind of hair oil doesn't work as well on your child's hair as it does on someone else's with the same hair type. The fun and challenge of working with textured hair is experimenting with it to find out what works best for each individual.

One More Hair Characteristic to Understand – Porosity

There is one more characteristic of your child's hair that you need to know: porosity. This term refers to each strand's ability to absorb and retain moisture.

Why is porosity so important?

Moisture is the key to healthy, beautiful hair. Yet, in textured hair the loopy or zigzag pattern of the hair prevents natural sebum from reaching the ends and moisturizing the hair, leaving the hair dry, thirsty and susceptible to damage and breakage. Therefore, Type 3 and Type 4 hair requires lots of moisture. The most effective moisturizers will vary based on the porosity of your child's hair (its ability to absorb moisture).

Hair porosity is determined by how tightly the hair cuticles—similar to roof shingles in appearance and function—are sealed. The cuticles can lay flat, stand wide open, or fall somewhere in between. The porosity of your child's hair determines which products and styling methods will deliver the most moisture to her strands and maintain it. Hair can have low, medium or high porosity. Let's examine each level of porosity and how it impacts your child's hair.

Low porosity hair: The cuticle lies flat, providing a tight seal that prevents moisture from penetrating the hair shaft. It is difficult for low porosity hair to absorb moisture.

Medium porosity hair: This is the ideal situation. Hair cuticles are lifted slightly, allowing moisture to penetrate the shaft. Yet, they are sealed enough to prevent the moisture from quickly escaping again. This type is the easiest to keep moisturized.

High porosity hair: Cuticles stand wide open. Hair with high porosity soaks up moisture like a sponge. However, since the "doors" never close, the absorbed moisture evaporates from the hair just as quickly. Strands are left dry and prone to breakage. High porosity hair is frequently the result of heat damage and chemical processing. This porosity level requires moisture daily.

Knowing whether your child's hair has low porosity, normal porosity or high porosity will help you to keep it moisturized and healthy. But how do you determine the porosity level of your child's hair?

The Sink or Swim Test: Here's a simple test to determine the porosity of your child's hair. Wash her hair, so it's free of products. Retrieve a strand of your child's naturally shed hair. It should have a tiny, white root bulb on one end; otherwise it is a broken hair. Drop the naturally shed hair into a glass of water.

If the strand remains at the top or sinks very, very slowly, it's because the strand isn't absorbing water. The hair has low porosity.

If the strand slowly drifts down, it's absorbing water at an optimal rate. The hair has medium, or optimal, porosity.

If the strand sinks to the bottom of the glass immediately, it's absorbing moisture too quickly. The hair has a high level of porosity and will have difficulty retaining moisture.

Why Hair Type Matters

We've established that there are no "good" or "bad" hair types; only different ones. So why is it important to know which hair type your child has?

Imagine that you were going to give your car an oil change. Would you walk into an automotive parts store and just request oil? You might try. However, before the clerk could recommend a product to you, he or she would need to know *the make and model of your car.* This information is essential because different cars require different grades of oil. Once the clerk understands the essential needs of your particular vehicle he can recommend a range of products to you within those parameters. The situation is quite similar when it comes to caring for your child's hair.

Learning your child's hair type and porosity level are the first steps to establishing a healthy hair routine.

Each hair type has very different needs. Once you understand your child's hair type and porosity level you will better understand those needs. Caring for your child's hair becomes easier.

Knowing the basic characteristics of your child's hair (fine and fragile; wiry and dry; wavy and slightly oily; low, medium or high porosity) will enable you to make suitable choices about the products and treatments that will work best for his or her hair. Within those parameters, trial and error is required to find the most effective hair products, the optimal hair care routine, and hairstyles that work best.

Now that we've explored the various types of textured hair, let's discuss why it's essential that you properly care for your child's hair and teach her to do so, too.

Chapter Four
The Importance of Properly Caring for Your Child's Hair

We've already learned about some of the characteristics that make your child's textured hair very different from yours. Textured hair tends to be more fragile, tangles more easily, and tends to be drier than straight hair. While textured hair may be coarser and appear stronger, it is actually more fragile than straight hair.

Your child's textured hair is delicate and must be cared for properly.

There are many reasons that you must learn to lovingly care for your child's textured hair. First, there's the obvious reason. Fragile hair requires tender-loving care in order to thrive and grow healthy. Using the wrong tools—like a small tooth comb or a brush with harsh bristles—will do more harm than good to your child's hair. Barrettes and headbands with jagged teeth, rubber bands, and ponytail makers with metal parts will also damage textured hair. Perhaps you've used these items in the past and noticed little bits of hair wrapped around the rubber bands or caught in the teeth of barrettes. These are broken hairs. The more you use these tools, the more breakage will occur.

Choosing the wrong styles for your child's hair type or making braids and ponytails too tight is not only painful for the child, it can do long-term damage to the hair and scalp. Traction alopecia occurs when the hair is repeatedly pulled too tightly. This frequently results in a "receding" hairline or bald patches. Improperly caring for your child's hair is serious. It can create irreversible damage.

Hurriedly combing your child's hair or trying to detangle dry, unprepared hair can cause significant damage to the hair and scalp.

Instead, create a hair care routine that allows you to groom for your child's hair in a relaxed environment that is pleasant for both of you. This brings us to another reason it's essential to care for your child's hair in a way that demonstrates your love and respect for the child **and** her hair.

How you care for your child's hair sends a clear message to your child.

The manner in which you care for and speak about your child's hair reveals how you feel about it. Use language that will make your child feel good about his hair, and he'll absorb this positive message. On the other hand, using derogatory terms sends a harmful message that will cause him to feel ashamed of, or at the very least, conflicted about his hair. This is damaging to the child's self-esteem and can have a negative impact on other areas of his life.

What if you don't use negative words to describe the child's hair, but you *dread* caring for it? Children are perceptive. They will quickly pick up on your unspoken feelings. If you're stressed and anxious about grooming your daughter's hair, she'll take her cue from you. She'll also be tense and stressed, making the experience miserable for both of you.

When daily hair care routines are dreaded by parent and child, a negative message is conveyed about the child's hair which she will internalize.

One mother discovered just how perceptive her four-year-old daughter was when she observed the little girl tugging on her doll's hair and sighing and groaning as she attempted to braid it. It broke the mother's heart to see that she'd taught her daughter to view her hair in a negative light—as a problem or nuisance that needed to be resolved.

Why does it matter whether or not your child has a positive relationship with her hair?

The relationship your child develops with her hair is inextricably linked to her self-image and confidence.

If your words and actions reveal your displeasure with caring for your child's hair, she will be deeply impacted by it. The four-year-old girl mentioned earlier had already begun developing a negative relationship with her hair, as evidenced by the way she treated her doll's hair. It's not difficult to understand why having a poor perception of one's hair, or any other physical feature, would trigger low self-esteem.

Such negative feelings are compounded if your child is the only person in her home, school or community who has kinky or curly hair. She already understands that she is different, but negative feelings about her hair will cause her to feel inferior to others who have "good" hair. Speak positively about your child's hair, and she will, too.

How you care for your child's hair doesn't just impact the perception she has of herself. It can also impact how others perceive you.

The appearance of your child's hair will impact how others perceive your ability to care for your child.

You love and care for your children, so unkind comments or looks of pity from other mothers regarding the state of your child's hair hurt. Often the person doesn't intend to be unkind. Perhaps they really do empathize with your situation. After all, any African-American mother with children of her own understands that caring for textured tresses can be challenging. If you've grown frustrated and simply left your child's hair to its own devices...well, we recognize that, too.

What if a child in your neighborhood frequently walked outside in his bare feet, even in cooler weather? Perhaps his face was always dirty and his clothes were tattered. Wouldn't you wonder if the child was receiving proper care?

This example may seem extreme in comparison to the state of your child's hair. Yet, others will likely perceive a child whose hair is always dry, tangled and knotted, dotted with lint, or whose scalp is dry and scaly in much the same way. If your child's hair isn't well-groomed, it reflects poorly on the child's caretaker. It can also be a source of embarrassment for the child.

On the other hand, when your child's hair looks good, he feels good, too. It gives him a sense of pride and buoys his self-confidence—an essential ingredient for success in school and in life.

This book will give you the tools and knowledge needed to make your child's hair care routine more enjoyable, and perhaps, an opportunity to bond. As you learn to care for your biracial or African-American child's hair, get her involved in the process as early as possible. This will help your child develop a healthy relationship with her hair.

Why is the life-long relationship biracial and African-American men and women have with their hair so important? Let's briefly examine the cultural significance of hair in the African-American community.

Chapter Five
The Cultural Significance of Hair in the African American Community

Hair has always had great social and cultural significance in African and African-American communities. In the book *Hair Story: Untangling the Roots of Black Hair in America*, authors Ayana D. Byrd and Lori L. Tharps review the history of black hair and reveal how that early history still impacts our perceptions today.

Among the African tribes from which the enslaved would later be taken, one's hairstyle revealed critical information about the individual. Byrd and Tharps state, "Within these cultures, hair was an integral part of a complex language system" (Byrd and Tharps, 2014).

Just how complex?

According to Byrd and Tharps, "[H]airstyles have been used to indicate a person's marital status, age, religion, ethnic identity, wealth, and rank within the community. In some cultures a person's surname could be ascertained simply by examining the hair because each clan had its own unique hairstyle" (2014).

One of the ways in which enslaved men and women were stripped of basic human dignities was by the forcible shaving of their heads. What impact did this act of aggression have on enslaved men and women arriving in the New World? "The shaved head was the first step the Europeans took to erase the slave's culture and alter the relationship between the African and his or her hair...Arriving without their signature hairstyles, [slaves] entered the New World, just as the Europeans intended, like anonymous chattel" (Byrd and Tharps, 2014).

Being forced into slavery in a strange land where they were stripped of nearly every human dignity, many deeply held tenets remained, including the significance of one's hair. Those held captive in slavery soon learned that their hair held great significance in their new land, just as it had in their native lands.

The article *Hey Girl, Am I More than My Hair?: African American Women and Their Struggles with Beauty, Body Image, and Hair* is a historical perspective on how differences in body image, skin color and hair impact the self-image of women of color living in a society that judges typical African-American features against a European aesthetic. Author Tracey Owens Patton states, "Since 1619, African American women and their beauty have been juxtaposed against White beauty standards, particularly pertaining to their skin color and hair." (2006) Not surprisingly, enslaved individuals with characteristics which more closely aligned with the European ideal of beauty (straighter, wavier hair and lighter skin) were deemed worth more at auctions and often held positions as house slaves.

Life as a house slave was by no means easy living. Yet, it afforded a far better situation than that experienced by slaves with dark skin and coarse hair who were forced to work in fields. No wonder this equation of having lighter skin and "good hair" making one "more valuable" was internalized by enslaved individuals and the generations of African-Americans who succeeded them.

Fast forward to where we are now. How does this historical information about the significance of hair to African tribes and enslaved Africans forcibly brought to America relate to the psychology and significance of hair to people of color today? After all, society has changed tremendously in the centuries since then. Hasn't it?

The historical facts have *everything* to do with the ongoing significance of hair to African-Americans and biracial individuals. Wearing one's hair in its natural state is rarely controversial for members of other racial groups. However, many African-American men and women struggle with whether or not they should wear their hair in the state in which it grows from their heads.

Why would wearing one's hair naturally be considered controversial?

Many institutions, like the business world and academia, often regard people of color who wear their hair naturally with distrust. They're viewed as rebels or labeled as "unprofessional". On the other hand, those who choose to alter their hair to a state that more closely aligns with society's standards of European beauty are considered conservative and "less threatening." The very act of wearing one's hair naturally is often viewed as making a political statement. In recent years there have been several instances in which schools and business organizations have banned natural hairstyles like braids, afro puffs and dreadlocks. Such harsh views of natural, textured hair are not limited to those outside of the African-American community.

Among people of color there are opposing views about the "appropriateness" of wearing one's hair in its natural state. Many of my clients who've chosen to go natural, after many years of chemically-straightening their hair, have been surprised to find that they have received the strongest censure regarding their new look *from other women of color*. Why? These women often share Corporate America's point of view about textured hair. They believe that natural hair looks unkempt and is "unprofessional". Some African-American men and women associate kinky, coily hair with slavery and therefore criticize those who embrace their natural hair.

With all of the negativity surrounding wearing one's kinky or curly hair in its natural texture, you might be inclined to believe that it would be easier for everyone involved if you simply straighten your child's hair. However, straightening your child's hair, simply because it is "different," may feel tantamount to rejecting an integral part of him or her. Rather than trying to erase what makes your child's hair different, this book will teach you how to ensure that your child's hair is healthy and looks its best, so that both you and she will be proud of her curly or kinky mane.

You won't be alone on this journey. There is a growing movement among people with textured hair of all ethnicities who are celebrating their waves, curls, coils and kinks. These individuals proudly embrace their textured locks and wear their hair in its natural state—with all that entails for each wearer. Consequently, a growing number of institutions within the corporate world and academia have come to recognize and accept natural hair.

Now that we understand the cultural significance of hair in the African American community, let's talk about how you can help your child to embrace this important part of her identity.

Chapter Six
Teaching Your Child to Embrace Her Natural Hair

Since European beauty standards have been set as the measure of what is beautiful for women everywhere, where does this leave the child that doesn't meet those standards? As you can imagine, this can deliver a devastating blow to such a child's self-esteem. However, that doesn't have to be the case for your child. Your diligence will expand your child's concept of beauty to one that is inclusive, rather than exclusive. Let's explore what you, as a parent, can do to help your child embrace her natural, textured hair and develop healthy self-esteem.

The Message Begins with You

Children are extremely observant. This begins at an early age. Through observation our children learn important life lessons, including what it is that we value in ourselves and others.

Just as children mimic our words and actions, they also tend to adopt our attitudes. So what attitudes are we conveying to our children regarding what constitutes beauty?

In an earlier chapter we discussed how the manner in which you care for your child's hair relays your true feelings about it. If you lovingly care for the child's hair and speak about it using positive language, the child receives a positive message about her hair. On the other hand, if you treat the child's hair roughly and speak disparagingly about the child's hair, that message is received loud and clear, too. So carefully consider the language you use to talk about natural hair. Reinforce those positive messages by patiently styling your child's hair. This demonstrates that you truly value her natural hair.

Negative messages about your child's hair don't have to be verbalized. Body language, facial expressions and sighs of frustration also convey that you find it difficult or unpleasant to deal with your child's hair. Children quickly soak up the unspoken intimation that their hair texture, and by extension, they themselves, fail to meet society's beauty standards.

A child bombarded with negative messages about her hair internalizes the belief that she has "bad hair." This is devastating to the child's esteem and can have lasting effects. A negative self-image developed as a child often stays with us as adults.

Take the time to tell your child that she is beautiful. The images she is bombarded with in magazines, television, and movies set a standard of beauty that may be very different from what she sees in the mirror. In the absence of a positive message asserting her value and beauty, she may arrive at the conclusion that she isn't beautiful.

Actively contradict pervasive societal messages which define beauty in a limited, exclusionary manner by speaking about and treating your child's hair it in a way that is positive and affirming.

Provide Positive Images of Textured Hair

Most images on television and in magazines cling to the notion that European beauty is the standard by which everyone must be measured. However, there is a growing number of positive images of men and women wearing textured hair in the media. How can you use these images to help your child embrace her natural hair? Here are a few simple ways to do this.

- Point out people of color with textured hair in television shows and commercials. Make genuinely positive comments like, "Look, she has beautiful, curly hair, just like yours."

- Buy toys and books that reinforce positive images of diverse, natural beauty.

- Purchase dolls/action figures with hair texture similar to your child's.

- Subscribe to magazines that portray positive images of diverse beauty.

Providing positive images of curly and kinky hair will counteract the implied media message that only straight, shiny hair is beautiful. This will help boost your child's self-esteem. However, there is a far more powerful example that is much closer to home.

Set the Example

Do you have textured hair, or is there something about your hair that drives you crazy? How do you treat *your* hair? Do you frequently lament that you can't do anything with it or that it isn't like your mother's (sister's, friend's, etc.)? If so, your child will be inclined to adopt the same attitude about her hair. Proper care demonstrates to your child that you embrace your hair. It also increases the likeliness that she will do the same.

As a busy mother, it can be difficult to find time to fulfill all of the duties inherent to our many, and often conflicting, roles. It isn't surprising that we frequently sacrifice time for self-care. However, making the time to properly care for our hair teaches our children that we value ourselves and embrace our own unique beauty. It is an important lesson that our children (especially our daughters) need to learn.

Teach Your Child to Properly Care for Her Hair

As soon as your child is capable, allow her to take part in her daily hair care routine. Teach your child how to properly care for his or her hair by explaining:

- The properties of his or her hair in positive terms.

- What products you use.

- Why certain products work best on the child's hair.

- Proper techniques for washing, conditioning, detangling and combing the child's hair.

- Basic styling techniques.

Providing your child with simple explanations for each step in his or her hair care routine is empowering. He will begin to feel like he is part of the process. This encourages his willing participation.

For instance, take a little girl who hates to have her hair tied up in a head scarf before bed each night. Explain to her that this is a very special scarf made to protect her hair while she's sleeping so that it will stay soft and beautiful. She may quickly experience a change of heart.

When you teach your child to respect her textured hair by properly caring for it, you are helping her to establish a lifelong positive relationship with her hair.

Set Realistic Expectations

One important aspect of developing a positive relationship with one's hair is to set realistic expectations. No matter how well one cares for Type 4B hair, it will never transform into 3A. Learn to love your child's hair with all of its quirks and help him or her to do the same.

As you expose your child to positive images of natural hair, be sure that she understands that her hair is unique. It won't necessarily behave like someone else's, even if their textures appear to be quite similar.

Teach your child to love and accept her textured hair, rather than comparing it to someone else's.

Now that you understand the physical properties of kinky and curly hair, the historical significance of one's hair in communities of color, and how to ensure that your child has a positive view of his or her hair, it's time to get down to the nuts and bolts of caring for your child's natural hair. In the next section, we'll explore the products you'll need to properly care for your child's textured hair.

Section II
What You'll Need

Chapter Seven
Use the Proper Styling Tools

When it comes to caring for your child's natural hair, think of yourself as both a doctor and an artist. The former is charged with maintaining health. The latter's precision and artistry appeal to the soul. However, neither can be successful without the proper tools.

To properly care for your child's hair, you will also need the proper tools. Here's a brief list of the basic hair care tools required to care for your child's hair, as directed in later chapters:

Wide Tooth Comb/Pick

The wide tooth comb is an excellent tool for detangling hair. Shown is the My Honey Child Cake Cutter Comb. With a four-inch handle and three-inches of four-inch wide teeth, this comb can easily detangle even the thickest locks.

Denman Brush

The Denman 7 Row Medium Styling Brush pictured is a perennial favorite among natural hair wearers. The wide spaces between the rows make it the perfect tool for detangling thick hair. Some users whose hair is especially thick have found it advantageous to remove every other row of bristles.

Rattail Comb

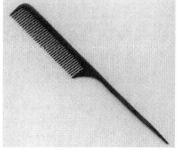

The rattail comb has a skinny, pointed handle that is particularly useful when it comes to styling your child's hair. Use the pointed handle to make clean, even, precision parts for styles like cornrows, twists and ponytails.

While the tail makes this comb appealing, the teeth are typically quite small. Don't ever be tempted to use the teeth of the rattail comb to comb your child's hair, as this will lead to breakage.

Spray Bottle

It is often easier to work with textured hair when it's damp. Keep a spray bottle, filled with water, on hand when styling your child's hair. Use the spray bottle to spritz moisture on your child's hair before combing or styling.

For an extra punch, use a mixture of two-thirds water and one-third aloe vera juice to moisturize your child's strands between washes. This mixture encourages your child's natural curl pattern while also reducing frizz. Alternately, you can add a bit of oil to the water. Experiment with different formulas to see what works best for your child's hair. If using as a moisturizer, immediately follow up with an oil or hair butter in order to seal in moisture.

A Few Other Useful Tools:

- **Hair Clips** – Use these to section hair while braiding or twisting. Be sure to get clips without jagged metal teeth which damage hair.

- **Ouchless ponytail holders** – Ponytails are frequently used as quick go-to styles for little girls. Choose ponytail holders that don't have metal clips or seams that will snag hair when removed.

- **Ribbons, Bows and Other Accessories** – Hair accessories like ribbons and bows can be used to embellish hairstyles. Select options that won't damage strands or put too much stress on the hairline.

- **Old Cotton T-shirt** – Cotton isn't an ideal material for your child's pillow case. However, a cotton t-shirt will quickly absorb excess water from your child's hair after washing.

- **Satin Bonnet or Scarf** – A satin scarf or bonnet protects textured hair from friction caused by harsh bedding fabrics which tend to dry out hair.

- **Satin Pillowcase (optional)** – A satin scarf won't stay in place all night if your child is a fitful sleeper. A satin pillowcase serves the same purpose. For maximum protection, use a satin scarf and a satin pillowcase.

The styling tools listed are available in drug stores, big box stores, and beauty supply stores. This is a basic list to get you started. You'll likely discover others. Next, we'll examine basic styling products you'll need to take care of your child's hair.

Chapter Eight
Essential Hair Products

Just as certain styling tools should always be on hand, there are several products that you'll want to keep stocked in your cabinet. We'll review the basic categories and briefly discuss the role each plays in the health and beauty of your child's hair.

You will discover that a variety of products are used to care for textured hair. These products are often layered to infuse the hair with moisture and seal it in the strands. Now, let's review some of the essential hair care products for healthy textured hair.

Hydrating, Sulfate-free Shampoo (Optional)

Most shampoos contain harsh sulfates which cause the suds that we've been taught to expect from our shampoos. Sulfates strip the hair of its natural oils. This can have devastating effects on curly and coily hair strands because the construction of the strands already makes it difficult for natural oils to travel down the hair shaft to the ends.

Harsh detergents aren't necessary to cleanse the hair. The primary job of shampoo is to cleanse the scalp. This can actually be achieved without the use of shampoo. We'll discuss this in more depth shortly.

If you choose to use shampoo on your child's hair, read labels carefully. Even "no-tears" shampoos frequently contain sulfates. Be on the lookout for ingredients like sodium lauryl sulfate, alkyl benzene sulfonate, ammonium lauryl sulfate and other similar ingredient names by which sulfates are often disguised.

Select hydrating shampoos that are sulfate-free. These products cleanse the hair and scalp without stripping the hair of moisture and altering its PH level. Hydrating shampoos add moisture to strands.

Clarifying Shampoo

The products used to condition and style your child's hair may eventually begin to leave a residue on the hair and scalp. This product build-up can make hair look dull and cause the scalp to feel dry and itchy. Use a clarifying shampoo once a month to avoid or eliminate product buildup.

Clarifying shampoos are harsher than regular, hydrating shampoos. For this reason, they do a thorough job of cleansing the hair of product buildup, chlorine and other residue. Unlike hydrating shampoos, they don't typically add moisture to the hair. Therefore, clarifying shampoos should not be used frequently, as this could be damaging.

Moisturizing Conditioner

Moisture is essential to the health of textured hair. Therefore, it's critical to select a moisturizing conditioner. Humectants help the hair to attract and maintain moisture. This can be especially beneficial for hair with low porosity. Light, water-based moisturizers penetrate tight cuticles more easily.

A good moisturizing conditioner can be used in its traditional role, to improve the condition of the hair following a shampoo wash. However, many naturals use a hydrating conditioner to wash their hair. This is called no-pooing or co-washing. The conditioner moisturizes the hair and helps cleanse the scalp.

Not every conditioner will work with every hair type. Finding the right conditioner for your child's hair will take some trial and error. If you don't like the results you're getting from your current conditioner, chuck it and try a different product.

Leave-in Conditioner

Textured hair requires some form of moisture almost daily. Many find a good leave-in conditioner to be helpful. Select a water-based, leave-in moisturizer that will easily penetrate the hair shaft instead of coating the strands and leaving them heavy or waxy. A good leave-in conditioner can be applied to damp hair after it's washed. It can also be used to give the hair an added boost of moisture in between washes.

Deep Conditioners

Curly and coily tresses are more fragile than straight hair, yet they tend to take more abuse. Daily styling and manipulation of the hair can strain already fragile strands to the limit, resulting in dry, brittle hair that easily snaps when combed or styled. Environmental factors also take their toll. In the summer, intense heat and sunlight can dry out textured hair. The dry, warm air circulating indoors during winter can also have a drying effect on kinky or curly hair, leaving it dull and lifeless.

Moisture is essential to healthy, textured tresses. Regular deep conditioning is an essential part of the hair care routine in order to achieve healthy textured hair and soft, shiny, bouncy curls. An effective, moisturizing deep conditioner hydrates dry, lifeless strands. As a result, the hair will be softer and have more elasticity. This reduces breakage while styling. Moisturizing conditioners are usually thick and creamy. An effective, moisturizing deep conditioner hydrates hair without weighing it down. A creamy, deep conditioner also provides great slip (slipperiness), which facilitates detangling.

However, to get the best results, it isn't enough just to coat hair with the product. The real work occurs at a much deeper level, when the deep conditioner penetrates the hair shaft. This permits essential hydration to reach the cortex of each strand, supplying it with vital nourishment. Applying gentle warmth lifts the cuticles, or outer layer of the hair, enabling the conditioner to reach the cortex underneath so strands can absorb moisture. In Chapter Ten, we'll discuss several methods for safely applying heat during deep conditioning.

If hair is weak and damaged, moisture alone may not be enough. You child's hair may be in need of a protein treatment. Some deep conditioners are designed to infuse damaged strands with a protein like keratin, which is the major component of hair, skin and nails. Such treatments strengthen the hair by reinforcing the structure of each strand. This repairs some of the damage to weakened strands while also smoothing them. Though protein can improve the health and appearance of the hair, too much of a good thing can have the opposite effect. Too much protein makes hair stiff and brittle. This makes strands susceptible to breakage.

Finding the proper balance of moisture and protein may take some trial and error. As a general rule, if the hair feels too soft or mushy when wet, a protein treatment is required. If the hair is dry and brittle, a deep conditioner is required. A good guideline is to deep condition your child's hair at least once each week. A protein treatment may be applied once a month. Adjust according to the needs of your child's hair.

Daily Moisturizer

The moisturizing routine isn't complete once you rinse the conditioner from your child's hair. Textured hair could use another shot of moisture and help to *maintain* that extra moisture. A good moisturizer easily manages both jobs. It introduces additional moisture to strands and then retains it. As with a moisturizing conditioner, a creamy consistency is also preferable when selecting a daily moisturizer.

Note about Humectants: Humectants are ingredients often used in moisturizing hair products. They attract moisture from the air and draw it into the cortex of each hair strand. This allows water molecules to bond with hair strands and retain vital moisture. Humectants commonly found in moisturizers can range from basic, organic ingredients like aloe vera juice and honey to glucose, glycerin and hydrolyzed proteins.

The leave-in conditioner or daily moisturizer you choose for your child's hair might be a humectant. Such products can contribute to bouncy, shiny curls that retain their shape. However, when the air is extremely humid, humectants can draw too much moisture into the hair strand. The result is big, poufy, frizzy strands that don't retain their curl pattern. Highly-porous strands are particularly susceptible to frizz in this situation.

In arid conditions, the extremely low amount of humidity can wreak havoc on strands coated with humectants. Since there is no moisture to draw from the air, the humectant draws moisture from the cortex of the hair—where it is most needed—to the surface. This can cause the hair to become dry and brittle and make strands susceptible to breakage.

Humectants can be an important component of your child's healthy hair routine, depending on the local climate and your child's hair type. Once you know the porosity level of your child's hair (see Chapter Three), it's easier to determine which products will likely work best. Use humectants when the air is neither too dry nor too humid. Pay attention to how your child's hair responds to humectants and adjust your routine accordingly.

Natural Oils and Hair Butters

Conditioners and a daily moisturizer can boost the hydration level of your child's hair and help retain moisture. However, thick, dry hair can still quickly lose moisture during the course of the day. Natural oils help seal in moisture, so that your child's hair stays soft and supple longer.

Avoid heavy oils as the primary source of moisture for your child's hair. Heavier oils don't penetrate the hair shaft. Instead, they sit on the surface of the hair, making it look and feel greasy. Using such oils can be counterproductive when they are used as the primary source of moisture for your child's hair. Heavy oils, which include mineral oil and petroleum-based "moisturizers," don't provide the vital moisture your child's hair needs. They further exacerbate dryness by sealing dry hair and preventing moisture from entering.

While mineral oil and petroleum-based products should be avoided, there are many oils that are beneficial for textured hair. Though most oils cannot penetrate the shaft to moisturize hair, some do have this capability. Coconut oil, olive oil, avocado oil and Argan oil are absorbed into the hair shaft. These oils can help moisturize the hair, especially when used to pre-poo your child's hair. (We'll discuss this method more in Chapter Nine.) Oils like castor oil, jojoba oil and grapeseed oil are excellent sealants which help your child's hair retain moisture when used as the final layer in your child's moisturizing routine. Products with mango or shea butter can also serve as excellent sealants when applied after water or a water-based moisturizing product.

In this section, we've covered essential hair products that you'll need to keep your child's hair healthy. There are countless shampoos, conditioners, hair oils and hair butters available in a variety of price ranges. Despite being formulated specifically for curly hair, not every product will work for your child's hair. Based on your child's hair type, thickness and level of porosity, select products that address the unique needs of his or her hair. Experiment with a variety of products. If you can't find a product that's right for your child's hair in one line of products, try another.

It's easy to lose track of which products you've tried and whether they worked. Use a journal or spreadsheet to make a running list of products you've tried and the results achieved. When you find a product you love, don't be afraid to stock up on it.

Introduce new products one at a time. If you add several products to your child's hair routine at once, it's difficult to know which product to applaud (or blame) for the results. If a particular product doesn't seem to work well on your child's hair, send it to the back of the shelf and try something else. No matter how good it smells, or how expensive it is, not every product is going to work for your child's hair. It doesn't mean that you've done something wrong, and it happens to all of us. (Just ask any woman who wears her hair natural to show you her collection of failed hair products.) However, this experimentation is necessary to find the combination of products that will provide the best results for your child's hair.

After reading this section of the book, you know which styling tools and types of hair products you'll need to properly care for your child's hair. Next, let's take a step-by-step look at basic hair care and styling best practices.

Section III
How to Care for Biracial and African American Children's Hair

Chapter Nine
Cleansing & Detangling Your Child's Hair

Shampooing hair isn't a particularly complicated process. So why are we dedicating an entire chapter to this seemingly simple task?

The unique characteristics of biracial and African American hair can make this process, and all others, a more challenging for someone who isn't accustomed to handling it. Every facet of cleansing can have an impact on the health and retention of your child's hair: your choice of shampoo, how the hair is handled during and afterward. Therefore, let's examine how to safely and effectively cleanse your child's hair in a way that will promote health, and if desired, length.

Shampooing vs. Co-washing

In the previous section, it was noted that some naturals prefer to use a moisturizing conditioner to cleanse their hair, rather than shampoo. We've been taught that lather is essential and that the hair should be "squeaky clean." So you may find it difficult to embrace the idea of replacing your child's shampoo with a conditioner. However, co-washing can be a very effective way to cleanse your child's hair and scalp.

Shampoos often use harsh sulfates which produce lots of lather as they cleanse the hair and scalp. However, in doing so, they strip the hair of essential oils. This is particularly devastating to textured hair, which already tends to be dry. The coiled pattern of textured hair makes it more difficult for natural oils to travel down the full length of the hair shaft. Therefore, it's harder for curly or coily hair to recover from a loss of essential oils.

Sulfate-free shampoos are gentler on your child's hair. However, co-washing can get the hair and scalp just as clean. The essential function of shampoo is to *cleanse the scalp*. This can be achieved by lubricating the scalp with a moisturizing conditioner and using the pads of the fingers (Not the fingernails!) to loosen dirt, oil and grime that have built up on the scalp. The hair and scalp both get cleansed, yet the hair isn't stripped of essential oils.

The added bonus? Your child's hair will retain more moisture, an essential component to healthy, beautiful hair.

Does that mean that shampoo has no place in your child's hair care regimen? No. There are times when shampooing is desirable. For instance, shampooing is preferable to:

- Remove heavy dirt and grime.

- Remove chlorine from your child's hair after swimming.

- Remove product buildup from the scalp.

- Clarify hair periodically.

Whether you choose to shampoo or co-wash your child's hair is a personal choice. However, if you've never co-washed your child's hair, it may be worthwhile to give it a test run. Try co-washing your child's hair for a month to experience the benefits for yourself. You'll likely find that her hair will be healthier, more hydrated, softer and suppler.

How Often Should Textured Hair be Shampooed?

Textured hair does not require daily shampooing.

The frequency with which you cleanse your child's hair will depend on how soiled it gets each day. For instance, a child who plays in a sandbox or at the beach daily may be the rare exception to the rule stated above. However, weekly shampooing or co-washing is a good starting point. Make adjustments based on your specific circumstances. For instance, in summer your child's hair may require cleansing twice each week due to sweat and grime from playing outside in warm weather. During other times of year, washing every other week may work best for your child's hair.

Step-by-Step Guide to Washing Your Child's Hair

Step One: Be thoroughly prepared.

Few children enjoy getting their hair shampooed. For children with textured hair, the hair care routine can easily become something they dread. Begin with the determination to change any negative perceptions your child may have about his or her hair care routine. Look for ways to make the process enjoyable for both of you. This begins with selecting the appropriate location for washing your child's hair.

Washing, detangling and conditioning your child's hair can be a rather lengthy process, especially if the child has long hair that tangles easily. Ensure that the setup you choose will be as comfortable as possible for both of you, throughout the entire process.

There are several steps to an effective wash day hair care routine for textured hair. Some steps will require that the child be at a sink or faucet. However, you may prefer to do some of the earlier steps elsewhere. Review the entire wash day hair care routine to decide which spot(s) in your home will work best. The ideal location for the hair care routine will vary from family to family, perhaps even from one child to another. There are many factors to take into consideration: Your child's age and personal preferences; the setup of your home; and what is most comfortable for you.

Pre-wash steps can be completed while the child is seated in your lap reading a book or on the floor in front of the television. The rinsing stages can be completed:

- At the bathroom sink, with the child standing on a stool.

51

- In the tub, during bath time.

- At the kitchen sink.

Bath time is often the ideal time to wash very young children's hair. For others, the kitchen sink may be the best option, especially if the kitchen sink has a convenient, detachable spray nozzle.

Once you've found the spot where you and your child will be comfortable for each stage of the process, it's time to ensure that you have all of the tools you'll need. These will include:

- A wide-tooth comb

- Hair oils for pre-wash treatment

- A plastic shower cap or disposable, plastic grocery bag

- A towel or old cotton t-shirt

- Sulfate-free shampoo (optional)

- Creamy, moisturizing conditioner

- Sink sprayer (or a large cup or pitcher)

Once you've gathered all of the tools and products you need to get the job done, it's time to think about ways to make the process as enjoyable as possible for your child.

Step Two: Keep Your Child Preoccupied

Your child will quickly become bored and restless during a lengthy hair care session. Plan ahead by finding ways to keep your child occupied. Special toys that are just for hair care time are a perfect distraction that will help keep young children preoccupied.

Character-shaped sponge, squirt or float toys can keep your child distracted throughout the hair care process and make hair care something the child looks forward to each week. Color-changing bath tub tablets, bath crayons and finger paints are other options for entertaining restless young children. For older children, a tablet or smartphone can create an anytime, anywhere viewing screen for their favorite show or movie. Once your plan to make shampooing pleasant for your child (and you) is in place, it's time to prepare your child's hair for cleansing.

Step Three: Pre-poo

It's still not quite time to break out the shampoo bottle. Cleansers can be harsh on the hair, so it's important to prepare your child's hair for cleansing. To get your child's hair in the best possible condition before washing, you'll need to prepare and apply a simple, pre-shampoo (pre-poo) treatment.

Why bother treating your child's hair before washing and conditioning? Pre-pooing helps seal moisture into your child's hair to reduce the amount lost during shampooing. It also softens hair, making it more manageable and easier to detangle. Pre-pooing fortifies the hair cuticle, preparing it for the rigors of washing and manipulation. It also nourishes the scalp.

There are a variety of pre-poo options, each with its own benefits. Here are a few:

- Extra virgin olive oil (EVOO) is an especially beneficial oil for textured hair. While it is heavy enough to coat the hair and seal in moisture, it's also one of the few oils with the ability to penetrate the hair shaft, supplying additional moisture. In addition to sealing moisture in the hair, EVOO reduces frizz and adds shine to textured hair.

- Coconut oil is a versatile oil that can be used on the hair and skin. Rich in vitamin E and lauric acid, coconut oil also has the power to penetrate the hair shaft, applying much-needed moisture. The protein in coconut oil also helps to strengthen hair and protect against damage. It smells wonderful and increases shine while reducing frizz.

- Grapeseed oil, rich in vitamin E and linoleic acid, strengthens the hair. It is light, odorless and non-greasy. Grapeseed can be especially useful in helping to reduce dandruff.

- Avocado oil, loaded with vitamins, proteins, nutrients and fatty acids, is nourishing to the hair and scalp. Light enough to penetrate the hair shaft, avocado oil moisturizes and strengthens hair while boosting shine.

All of the oils listed above can be purchased in your local grocery or health food store. Each oil can either be used alone, in combination, or as a carrier oil, blended with other ingredients like castor oil or a few drops of an essential oil, like tea tree oil. If you aren't sure where to begin, EVOO is a good option.

In an earlier section, you assessed the texture and particular needs of your child's hair. Choose a pre-poo treatment that addresses any areas of concern, like dryness of the hair or scalp. Experiment with different pre-poo treatments to get the best results for your child's hair.

Once you've prepared the pre-poo you'll use on your child's hair, it's time to apply. Carefully section dry hair into four or five twists. Leave the last twist undone and begin with this section of hair. Take the pre-poo treatment and slather it onto the child's hair, starting at the ends and working your way toward the scalp. Work the oil through the section of hair, then twist the hair. Move to the next section. Take down the twist, apply oil to this section in the same manner as before. Re-twist the hair, then move to the next section, until the entire head of hair has been treated.

After you've applied the pre-poo treatment to your child's hair, put a plastic shower cap on the child's hair. Wrap a towel or old t-shirt around the plastic cap to seal in heat and prevent oil from escaping the cap. Allow the oil to penetrate the child's hair for at least thirty minutes. Now it's time to go to the next step: detangling.

Step Four: Detangle

Detangling your child's hair prior to cleansing is a critical step. It's important to the long-term health and length of your child's hair. A moisturizing, fortifying pre-poo treatment will make your child's hair stronger and suppler. It will also give the hair more slip, making it easier to detangle your child's hair while reducing the amount of breakage. The detangling process removes tangles, knots and bits of shed hair that hook themselves around the weakest portion of healthy hair—the bending or twisting sections. If these shed hairs aren't removed prior to washing, those knots tighten around healthy hair and cause breakage during cleansing and make detangling afterward a nightmare for you and your child. It can be tempting to skip this step, but don't give in to the temptation. Skip detangling and every part of your child's haircare routine that comes afterward will be twice as difficult for both of you while also increasing the likelihood of breakage and hair damage. Definitely not worth the risk!

Since your child's hair is already sectioned into twists from the pre-poo step, you'll take down one twist and work on a single section at a time. Prepare a spray bottle with one part oil—olive oil or coconut oil work well. Then add three parts water and shake it up. Spray this mixture on the hair, as needed, in order to keep the hair soft and supple enough to safely detangle. First, carefully work out knots with your fingers. If you find it difficult to slip the knots and tangles out without snapping off strands of hair, try saturating the section with a conditioner that provides great slip. Once you've worked out the knots and tangles, finish the process using a seamless wide tooth comb. Hold hair a few inches above the ends and begin detangling the ends of the hair first. Patiently work your way up the hair shaft, always holding the hair above where you are detangling to reduce stress on the strands. If you run into a particularly knotted section, add more of the water and oil mixture and patiently work through the knotted hair with your fingers. Then go back to using the comb. Don't yank the comb through tangled hair, as this will cause tangles to snap off, damaging the hair. Once a section has been thoroughly detangled, re-twist the hair and move on to the next section. Now that your child's hair has been completely detangled, it's finally time to begin shampooing (or co-washing) your child's hair.

Step Five: Shampoo or co-wash hair.

Continue to work in sections as you go to the next step. Take down one twist at a time. Rinse the hair, then saturate it with a sulfate-free shampoo or your cleansing conditioner of choice. No tears baby shampoos aren't recommended for biracial and African-American hair. While gentle on the child's eyes, these shampoos tend to be too harsh on textured hair. A moisturizing, sulfate-free shampoo is better than a no tears shampoo. Cleansing with a moisturizing conditioner is the most preferable option. Concentrate on cleansing the child's scalp, using the pads of your fingertips. Avoid using fingernails which can cause small wounds on the scalp. Tiny scratches on the scalp can get infected. These wounds can also exacerbate any dryness of the scalp that the child may already be experiencing.

Massage shampoo or conditioner into the hair. Even if you decide to co-wash, which is highly-recommended, there is no need to worry that your child's hair won't get clean. Most conditioners contain cleansing agents. Those cleansing agents combined with the gentle massaging of the hair and scalp will loosen dirt and debris. Massage the entire scalp, including the hairline and the nape of the neck. Once you've massaged the child's scalp and all of her hair, from the roots to the ends, the hair should be nice and clean. You're not looking for a "squeaky" clean, which usually indicates that the natural oils have been removed from the hair. You just want to ensure that all dirt has been removed and that the child's hair and scalp are clean and fresh. Rinse hair with lukewarm water until the water runs clear. A shower or sink spray nozzle attachment can be especially helpful during this step.

As outlined earlier, shampoo may be required occasionally. Here are a few situations which might require shampooing:

- When your child's hair is particularly dirty, like after a day at the beach or playground.

- To remove chlorine after a day at the pool.

- When product buildup is evident on hair and/or scalp.

In the instances listed above, a good clarifying shampoo is recommended. Since shampoo can be quite drying to the hair, your next step should be to apply a moisturizing deep conditioner to your child's hair to help replenish the moisture lost. Deep conditioning, as a next step after co-washing, is also recommended if your child's hair is dry or damaged. If you plan to deep condition the child's hair, the hair should remain wet after cleansing.

However, if you've co-washed your child's hair and you plan to style it as your next step, begin by gently wringing excess moisture from the child's hair. Next, grab an old cotton T-shirt or a microfiber towel. There are a wide range of microfiber towels designed specifically for drying natural hair. Wrap the towel or T-shirt around the child's head and squeeze gently squeeze each section, absorbing excess moisture. Do not rub the towel back and forth over the child's hair. This creates damaging friction that will disrupt your child's natural curl pattern and cause the hair to frizz. Instead, dab or blot the hair with the towel. Another option is to wrap the towel around the child's head and secure. Allow yourselves a short break while the towel absorbs the excess moisture. However, don't let the hair get too dry. Clean, damp hair will give you the best results when styling your child's hair. Now you're ready to prepare your child's hair for styling by moisturizing.

Chapter Ten
The Secret to Healthy, Beautiful Natural Hair—
Moisturizing and Conditioning

Throughout the book I've stressed how vital moisture is to maintaining healthy, beautiful natural hair. Since biracial and African-American hair tends to be drier, keeping your child's hair moisturized will require an ongoing, concerted effort. Later in this chapter, we'll talk about how to create a daily moisturizing routine. But first, let's begin with wash day moisturizing.

Conditioner Basics

If you choose to shampoo your child's hair, and a deep conditioner isn't required, follow up with a moisturizing conditioner. Select a hydrating conditioner, rather than a reconstructing conditioner. Designed to repair heavily-damaged hair, reconstructing conditioners typically contain heavy doses of protein. Unless your child's hair has been chemically-treated, a hydrating conditioner should suffice. Look for conditioners that infuse the hair with moisture and provide "slip." This will help reduce tangling and make it easier to comb and style your child's hair.

If you co-wash your child's hair, you'll be using a lot of conditioner. Don't break the bank right out of the gate. First, try an inexpensive, moisturizing conditioner. If an inexpensive, national brand works well, make it your go-to product for weekly co-washing or conditioning. Alternately, you may discover that your child's hair thrives on a higher-end, salon-quality conditioner, making it well worth the investment.

If you plan to deep condition your child's hair, skip the instant conditioner after shampooing. Go right into deep conditioning instead.

Infuse Moisture by Deep Conditioning

Deep conditioning is an essential part of your child's healthy hair routine. There are a wide variety of deep conditioners designed to give hair added hydration. In addition to a more hydrating formulation, deep conditioner is left on the hair much longer. This allows the conditioner to penetrate deeper.

If you pre-pooed the child's hair, as described in the last chapter, you've already given your child's hair a moisturizing boost. After cleansing the hair, preferably by co-washing, it's time to use a deep, moisturizing conditioner.

Apply the conditioner in sections, as you did when washing your child's hair. Work the deep conditioner into your child's hair. Either finger comb the conditioner through each section of the hair or rake a wide tooth comb through each section to ensure even distribution. The hair should be saturated with conditioner, from the scalp to the ends.

When the deep conditioner has been evenly applied to a section, retwist the hair and move on to the next section. Once deep conditioner has been applied to the child's entire head, cover the hair with a plastic shower cap.

Allow the deep conditioner to remain in the child's hair for twenty minutes to an hour. If the child's hair is especially dry or damaged, applying heat will help maximize results. Heat encourages the hair shaft to open, permitting the conditioner to penetrate deeper.

Heat can be applied using one of two methods. The first option is to wrap a heated towel around the plastic bag on the child's head. Leave the towel on for at least thirty minutes. The heat from the towel will allow the conditioner to permeate the hair shaft. Alternately, a hooded dryer can be used to get maximum results. Sit the child under a hooded dryer for twenty minutes. Be careful not to turn the setting up too high.

Once the deep conditioning is done, remove the plastic cap. Rinse hair with cool water. The cooler (Not cold!) temperature encourages hair cuticles to close, retaining moisture that was infused into the hair shaft during deep conditioning.

The recommended frequency of deep conditioning depends upon the health and texture of your child's hair. If the hair is especially dry, deep condition once a week. Type 4 and low porosity hair requires frequent deep conditioning. Type 3 hair may require less frequent deep conditioning. If the child's hair is healthy and retains moisture well, deep conditioning may only be necessary once a month.

You will need to experiment with various deep conditioners to discover which deep conditioner works best for your child's hair. If you've tried various products and homemade recipes, but still nothing seems to work, it may be time to turn to a professional. Consult with a natural hair specialist to ensure your child's hair gets needed hydration. During the appointment, talk with the stylist about your child's hair. Review your hair routine and explain any particular concerns. Request a recommendation for a deep conditioner. Ask why she recommends that particular product. This will help you to better understand your child's hair and make informed choices about other products and styles. Another option is to book appointments with a natural hair stylist for periodic deep conditioning treatments.

Leave-in Conditioner

Since moisture is key to keeping your child's hair healthy and supple, you'll want to add a conditioner that will remain in the child's hair. Regular and deep conditioners are designed to do their work and then be rinsed from the hair. However, as the name implies, leave-in conditioners are not rinsed from the hair after application. They provide the hair with a boost of additional moisture and create a barrier which helps to retain moisture. A good leave-in conditioner provides additional hydration, softens the hair and helps to counteract dryness, which can cause breakage.

Leave-in conditioners should be water-based, meaning that water is the first ingredient in the product. The leave-in conditioner may be a light, watery product that gets sprayed on the hair. Others are creamier and must be worked through the hair. If you are using a creamy leave-in conditioner, be sure to leave the hair fairly damp before applying. Work the leave-in conditioner through the hair in sections to ensure thorough, even coating. This helps retain moisture.

You might be wondering why you can't just leave your child's regular conditioner in her hair, rather than purchasing an additional product. Some naturals do leave regular conditioner in their hair. However, this isn't typically recommended for two reasons. First, regular and deep conditioners are heavier and can create product build-up if used as a leave-in conditioner. Second, a regular conditioner is formulated to deposit some ingredients in the hair while the rest is rinsed away. When those remaining components aren't rinsed from the scalp it can cause the scalp to feel tight and itchy. Therefore, a conditioner formulated as a leave-in is preferable.

LOC in Moisture

Not only is maintaining moisture in the hair an ongoing battle, it also requires a multi-pronged approach. That means layering products in textured hair to achieve the desired results. Many naturals use a method called LOC or LCO. The "L" stands for either liquid or leave-in, which was covered above. The water left from washing your child's hair, combined with the water-based leave-in conditioner comprise the first line of defense in retaining moisture. The next step is dependent upon your child's hair type. The "O" stands for oil and the "C" stands for cream (or hair butter). Try adding oil as the next step in the process. Lastly, add a cream or butter while styling to seal in moisture (both steps are covered in more detail later). However, if the LOC method doesn't work well for your child's hair, try flipping the last two steps in the process by adding a creamy daily moisturizer as the second step, then adding a natural oil as the final step.

Because you are using three different products, it will take some trial and error to figure out whether problems lie in the order chosen—LOC vs LCO—or the particular products being used. For instance, the type of cream or hair butter being used might be too heavy for your child's hair. Or perhaps your child's hair responds better to EVOO than to coconut oil. When possible, consider trying a product or method for a month before switching. This will give you a clearer picture of whether or not the product or method is right for your child's hair. Also, some products don't play well with others. So the problem may not lie in any single product, but in the way they react to each other. Product experimentation can be frustrating, but it can also be lots of fun. So enjoy the process as you discover what works best for you and your child.

Penetrating Hair Oils

While most oils sit on top of the hair shaft, weighing it down, in Chapter Eight we discovered that a few oils have the power to penetrate the hair shaft. By way of quick review, those oils include coconut oil, olive oil, avocado oil and argan oil. The molecular composition of these oils enables them to pass through the cuticle and into the cortex of the hair shaft. That makes these natural oils ideal for boosting moisture. The results you'll get using each of these oils on your child's hair may be vastly different.

For instance, some naturals rave about the amazing results they get by using coconut oil to seal the ends after the hair has been washed and moisturized. However, others have found that while coconut oil works wonders as a pre-poo for their hair, it wreaks havoc on their strands when used as a sealant. This is particularly true if the hair is "protein sensitive." Coconut oil prevents protein from escaping the hair shaft. The additional protein then causes hair to become dry and brittle, snapping off easily.

You'll discover the best oils for your child's hair through experimentation. However, a good starting point would be to use oils recognized for their ability to help retain moisture. Castor oil, jojoba oil and grapeseed oil are often used for this purpose.

Choosing the Right Hair Cream/Hair Butter

If you are following the LOC method, applying a good hair cream or hair butter will be the final step before styling the child's hair. If your child's hair is fine or porous, adding an additional product may be too much, making it look greasy and limp. If your child's fine or porous hair can tolerate this additional step, use the cream or butter sparingly.

Mango butter and shea butter can be effective sealants when combined with a carrier oil. Another option is to select a product like MYHONEYCHILD TYPE 4 Hair Crème, which offers a good balance of butters and oils. Emulsify the product between your hands before applying. If your child's hair tolerates the chosen product well, you can add a little more, as needed. Don't apply too much product. The hair should look shiny and healthy, but it shouldn't feel greasy.

If your child has coarse, thick hair, a heavier butter or cream may work best. Coarse, thick hair tends to get extremely dry, putting precious strands at risk of damage and breakage. Alleviate this tendency by using a heavy hair butter or cream. Always apply the product to damp tresses.

This helps seal in moisture, making coarse hair softer and suppler. Heavy butters and creams also reduce frizz and make coarse, thick hair more manageable.

Provide Daily Moisture

Before we move to styling, let's address the ongoing need to moisturize African-American and biracial hair. No matter how well the hair is moisturized during your wash day routine, it will need to be re-moisturized frequently. This is normal for African-American and biracial hair. However, if the moisturizing routine you've established works especially well, you may be able to moisturize your child's hair every few days. However, African-American and biracial hair typically benefit from daily moisturizing.

Which daily moisturizer should you use?

A water-based, daily moisturizer works based. There are many daily moisturizers to choose from that list water as the first ingredient. An alternate option is to make a simple mixture of two parts water and one part aloe vera juice. Spritz the mixture on your child's hair daily, immediately followed by your favorite oil, cream or butter. Alternately, a creamy, water-based moisturizer can hydrate hair and seal in moisture in a single step. As always, experiment with a variety of products until you find the one that works best for each child's hair. (What works well for one of your children might not necessarily work well for another.) Allow your knowledge of your child's hair type, texture and porosity to guide your selections. If you consult a natural hair stylist, request recommendations for a daily moisturizer for your child's hair, too.

Carefully read product labels before you make a purchase. Just as sulfates should be avoided in shampoos, alcohol should be avoided in moisturizers and conditioners. Alcohol is extremely drying when used on textured hair. Many of the moisturizers on the shelves in the ethnic hair care section of drugstores and big box stores have mineral oil or petrolatum among the most prominent ingredients. While many in the natural hair community that these two ingredients should be avoided, have discovered that their hair seemed drier and less supple without these ingredients in their hair products.

Mineral oil and petrolatum, byproducts of crude oil, aren't biodegradable. Both products are heavy and create a thick coating on hair that can be difficult to remove on wash day. In fact, the use of a sulfate shampoo may become a necessity if hair is slathered with a thick petrolatum product. I suggest that clients avoid mineral oil and petrolatum products initially. Instead, stick to products that have natural oils and butters. If softness and suppleness cannot be achieved using natural oils and butters, try a product that contains mineral oil. However, look for products that don't list mineral oil or petrolatum as the first ingredient.

Through trial and error, you'll discover whether your child's textured hair is better off with or without mineral oil and petrolatum products. If you've resorted to mineral oil products and your child's hair is still dry, unmanageable and prone to breakage, make a consultation appointment with a natural hair stylist. The knowledge you'll gain during this appointment can save time, money and frustration for you and your child in the years to come.

Protect Moisture Overnight

The quest to protect your child's hair and maintain vital moisture doesn't end at bedtime. Overnight, while your child is sleeping, her hair could be damaged by the fabric of her pillow. Cotton absorbs the moisture in hair. This tendency makes a cotton T-shirt ideal for drying excess moisture from the hair on wash day. Yet, it can be disastrous while your child is sleeping. The cotton pillowcase robs hair of moisture, drying it out. The friction of your child's hair rubbing against the cotton as she sleeps (especially if she is a restless sleeper) further damages the hair and can contribute to breakage.

To protect your child's hair, tie a silk or satin scarf around your child's hair and/or put a satin sleep cap on her head. Put the sleep cap on inside out so that the seam doesn't damage the hairline. If your child doesn't like sleeping with a scarf or cap on her head, invest in a satin pillow case. The sleek fabric allows your child's hair to glide along the fabric while she sleeps, without causing damage or sapping moisture from her hair. A doo rag can be used to protect little boys' hair while they sleep. Just make sure that the band of the doo rag isn't too tight. If so, it could cause a permanent line across the forehead. Sleep caps and doo rags can be found in any beauty supply store or the ethnic hair section of most drug stores or big box stores.

African-American and biracial hair tends to be dry. So if your child's hair is dry, don't panic. This is typical. Replenishing the moisture to your child's hair will require a concerted, ongoing effort. Make moisturizing a priority in your child's daily hair grooming routine. Doing so will, in large part, determine the health of your child's hair.

One of the reasons it is so important to keep your child's hair moisturized is to ensure that the hair is healthy, supple and easy to manage. This will make the next step—combing and styling your child's hair—much easier.

Chapter Eleven
Combing and Brushing African American and Biracial Hair

The battle to comb and style your child's hair is probably what prompted you to pick up this book. The fragile, dry nature of curly and coiled hair can make combing and styling challenging. When not done properly, styling is no picnic for your child either. Yet, as discussed in earlier chapters of this book, with proper care, combing and styling your child's hair will become much easier. But before we deal with *how* to safely comb your child's hair, let's address *why* we comb textured hair.

Combing (or finger combing) textured hair removes tangles, lint and other debris. It may also be necessary to coax strands into a certain style. However, combing curly hair breaks up the natural curl pattern. Curls can lose their definition and the hair may become frizzy. Therefore, prepping the hair before combing provides the best results.

Textured hair is softer and suppler when it's been moisturized. It's easier to comb and style. Moisture is an ongoing need for curly hair, and it is essential when it comes to styling your child's hair.

I caution my clients to never comb their children's textured hair when it's dry. In this state, the hair is fragile and vulnerable to damage and breakage. Particularly when improper tools are used. Protect your child's hair from unnecessary damage. Don't comb or style the hair while it is completely dry.

It is much more difficult to comb and detangle dry hair, making damage inevitable. Instead, grab your handy bottle of water and aloe vera juice. Spritz your child's hair, and distribute moisture throughout the hair, including the crown, back and nape. If the child's hair is thick, lift sections of hair so that the sections underneath receive an even coating of moisture, too.

Add a leave-in conditioner. Work the product through hair thoroughly. The child's hair should be damp when you're done, but not soaking wet. Now, use a seamless, large-tooth comb to work through the child's hair in sections, removing any stubborn tangles. Begin at the ends, working your way through any tangles patiently.

Hold the section of hair just above where you're combing. Work your way up the section until you are able to comb the hair from the roots to the ends without snags. Starting at the ends will prevent yanking of the hair, which is painful for the child, especially if he or she has a tender scalp. This also prevents damage.

If a section of hair dries before you get to it, rewet the section before combing and detangling it. For hair that is especially thick or porous, focus on one section at a time. Spritz, comb and detangle that section. Then move on to the next and repeat.

Observe the hair as you comb it. Are broken hairs collecting in the comb? Listen as you comb your child's hair. Does the hair sound rough and dry, like hay? Rewet the hair or use a leave-in conditioner with more slip. If you hear popping and snapping sounds, strands are being broken and torn during combing. Check the comb for seams, which snag the hair. Take your time and comb the hair gently. If a section of the hair is especially tangled, finger detangle the hair first.

Once you've removed tangles with a large tooth comb, use a rattail comb to create parts, as needed, for the hairstyle you've selected. For a center part, start at the hairline above the center of your child's forehead. Gently press the tail of the comb there. Slowly make a part down the middle, detangling, if needed. Once you've created a neat part down the center, use a ponytail maker or clip that is safe for natural hair to secure one section of the child's hair. Then begin at the center of the crown and use the same method to create a part that culminates behind the child's ear. Secure each section, then repeat on the other side.

This will create four sections, allowing you to begin any number of styling techniques from ponytails and afro puffs to braids and two-strand twists. If your child's hair is particularly thick or hard to manage, create more sections. This will give you smaller, more manageable zones. Working with more sections will make the process lengthier. However, it will make the process easier for you and your child. Just use one of the distraction techniques we discussed earlier to keep your child preoccupied.

Allow ample time to comb and style your child's hair. Rushing through the process will guarantee misery for both of you and damage your child's hair.

Daily grooming is required. Daily combing isn't.

Textured hair differs from straight hair in the frequency with which it requires combing. Even a wide tooth comb can cause mechanical damage to fragile, natural hair. To promote the health and length of your child's hair, try to style the child's hair in a manner that eliminates the need for daily combing. Such hairstyles are called protective hairstyles, because they protect curly and coiled hair from the need for daily combing and other manipulation which can be damaging. (We'll cover a variety of protective hairstyles in Chapter Fifteen). Short, textured hair (a few inches in length or less) can be combed daily with minimal damage. However, as curly hair gets longer, daily combing can be problematic. The texture and length of your child's hair and the style in which it is worn will dictate how frequently it should be combed and detangled between wash days. Especially with short or wash and go styles, finger combing or finger styling may suffice.

What about brushing your child's hair? Perhaps as a young child you were taught to brush your hair one-hundred strokes every night before bed to keep your hair shiny and healthy. Brushing straight hair does have its benefits. The brush stimulates blood flow to the scalp, redistributes oil from the scalp to the ends of the hair and removes debris. However, one-hundred strokes is overkill, even for straight hair. Overzealous brushing or using the wrong brush can have a devastating effect on curly or coiled hair.

There are a variety of brushes available. Not all of them will work well for your child's hair. Boar bristle brushes have soft bristles that can help smooth the cuticle of the hair. This makes boar bristle brushes ideal for smoothing down the edges of your child's hair. For instance, a boar bristle brush is helpful when creating ponytails or other styles where you want to get a smooth look around the edges. Boar bristle brushes also help stimulate the scalp and increased blood flow. When the child's hair is parted, a boar bristle brush can be used close to the scalp along the parts. If your child's hair is cropped close to the scalp, the boar bristle brush can be used all over the head to stimulate the scalp. However, do not use a boar bristle brush on wet hair, as this can cause damage. The hair should be dry or only slightly damp.

When purchasing a boar bristle brush, look for one with all-natural bristles. Avoid brushes with synthetic fillers, as these fibers can damage the hair.

Another brush that can be useful is the Denman brush. There is a wide selection of Denman brushes. The Denman Classic Styling Brush has smooth, rounded nylon bristles that are generously spaced to facilitate detangling. The Denman Classic Styling Brush can be used after pre-pooing the hair (when dry hair has been saturated with oils) or after co-washing to detangle hair.

Detangle your child's hair with a Denman brush by first parting the hair into sections. As always, begin detangling hair gently at the ends. Slowly work your way up toward the scalp as you continue to remove tangles.

Combing your child's hair properly will help prepare the hair for styling, keep the hair well-groomed and reduce the occurrence of knotting and tangles. Brushing your child's hair keeps the scalp healthy by encouraging blood flow and smooths edges. Though daily combing isn't a necessity, daily grooming is essential. Keeping your child's hair well-groomed is an important part of building the child's self-esteem and encouraging the child to develop a healthy self-image.

Now that you've combed and brushed your child's hair, it's time to take a look at another important hair hygiene step that will help keep your child's hair healthy and strong—trimming the ends.

Chapter Twelve
Promote Healthy Hair with Regular Trims

As the ends of the hair age, they begin to show signs of wear. Dry, damaged ends and split ends can wreak havoc on hair, if not addressed in a timely manner. This is just as true for children as it is for adults. Removing damaged ends, also called trimming the ends, is an essential part of any good natural hair care routine. But at what age should you begin trimming your child's hair? And how often should ends be trimmed?

Your child's hair should first be trimmed when he or she is around two and a half to three years of age, depending on your child's hair and his or her level or preparedness. While there are no hard and fast rules as to how frequently you should trim your child's ends, trimming the hair every three months is a good baseline. The health and condition of your child's hair will indicate when the ends need to be trimmed.

What are the signs that hair needs a good trim? Take a look at the ends of your child's hair. Can you see through the ends? This is likely a sign of split-ends (single strands of hair that are splitting up the shaft). If left unchecked, the strand will continue to split, compromising the entire strand. Split ends make hair feel dry and brittle. Often, split ends are caused by the incorrect use of styling tools or rough handling of the hair. Heat tools, like blow dryers, hot combs, flat irons and curling irons, are often the root cause of split ends. Chemicals like relaxers, Brazilian Keratin treatments and texturizers can also compromise the hair, creating split ends.

Single strand knots are another sign that ends need trimming. This occurs when a single strand of hair gets knotted on itself. You'll notice small balls of hair at the end of a single strand. Single strand knots are tough to detangle, and it you get frustrated and yank on it, the hair will snap, encouraging more split ends.

If the goal is to retain the length of your child's hair, trimming the ends regularly may seem counterproductive. Keep two things in mind. First, a trim isn't a haircut. The purpose of a trim is to remove the split ends, not reshape the hair. This usually only requires snipping a half an inch or so of the hair. Second, removing split ends keeps the hair healthy, a key factor in encouraging growth. On the other hand, damaged, split ends tend to break off faster than your child's hair can grow. Keeping the hair trimmed is one of the best things you can do to retain length.

If your child's hair is chemically-treated, you may find that her hair requires trimming every six to eight weeks. Natural, chemical-free strands that are kept moisturized and conditioned may only require trimming every few months. Hair that is neat and trimmed is less likely to tangle and easier to style.

While trimming the ends is vital to the health of the hair, the hair can be further damaged if trimming is done incorrectly. For instance, improper or dull scissors can cause more damage. Therefore, I do not recommend that parents trim their children's hair at home. This is one of the services that is best left to a trained, professional stylist. However, don't take your child to just any stylist. Look for a professional who is experienced working with African-American and biracial hair. The ideal option is to take your child to a natural hair stylist for trims and haircuts.

Chapter Thirteen
Hot Topic – The Hazards of Using Heat Styling Tools to Lengthen Hair

We've established that working with natural African-American and bi-racial hair can be more challenging than caring for straight hair. For some, the easier solution is to modify the structure of the natural hair using heat or chemicals.

Taming unwieldy kinks and coils with a straightening comb or relaxer may make strands look and behave more like the glossy, straight, European hair that our culture presents as being the standard of beauty. However, doing so can send a negative message to the child regarding the worth of her natural hair. Worse, using such means to straighten hair can cause irrevocable damage to the hair and scalp. Later, we'll discuss the straight truth about chemically-straightening your child's hair. First, let's examine the impact heat styling tools can have on your child's hair, best practices for safe use of these tools and effective alternatives to heat styling tools.

Hand-held blow dryers are used frequently to quickly dry the hair. If your child's hair is long and thick, you may opt for the convenience of a blow dryer to speed up the drying process. While some naturals do use a blow dryer as part of their regular hair care routine, such heat styling tools can be damaging to hair if not used properly.

If you choose to blow dry your child's hair, the best option is a hooded dryer. A quality hooded dryer is preferable because the warm air it generates heats up slowly during the half hour or so that your child sits under the dryer. This prevents hair from getting too hot, which can cause permanent damage to strands. A hooded dryer can even be used to infuse additional moisture in the hair. This can be achieved by putting a deep conditioner on the hair, placing a moisturizing cap on the child's hair and allowing her to sit beneath the dryer for thirty minutes or so. The hooded dryer can also speed up the drying time of a wash and go or protective styles like two strand twists. However, there may be times when you'd prefer to use a blow dryer to diffuse the hair or to create a blowout. If so, it's important to choose your heat styling tool wisely.

Low-priced blow dryers often have DC (direct current) motors and tend to have fewer speeds and temperature settings. Such tools can cause severe damage to your child's hair. Invest in a blow dryer that has at least three heat settings, including a cool setting, at least three speeds and an AC motor of 1875 watts.

Hair dryers with ionic, ceramic or tourmaline technology (or a combination of these) tend to be safer for natural hair. Ceramic blow dryers generate an infrared heat that dries hair gently. The heat is distributed more evenly so that a single section of the hair won't sustain damage by getting too hot. Ionic dryers generate negative ions which break down water droplets. This helps to dry hair more quickly. Tourmaline hair dryers incorporate a semi-precious stone that generates negative ions. These blow dryers emit negative ions and infrared heat to produce a quicker dry that is easier on tresses while boosting shine and reducing frizz.

Advanced blow dryer technology doesn't have to break the bank. Several models are available for around $40 or less that incorporate ceramic, ionic and tourmaline technology, several temperature settings and multiple speeds.

High-end blow dryers are gentler on hair. Yet, blow drying can still cause damage. Protect your child's hair by blowdrying no more than once or twice a month.

As always, you'll want to make sure to prep your child's hair for the best results. Begin with hair that is clean and freshly shampooed. Before blow drying, give your child's hair a good deep conditioning to infuse the hair with moisture. After your usual detangling routine, dry the hair with a cotton T-shirt, then apply a leave-in conditioner that can also double as a heat protectant. If your leave-in conditioner isn't capable of fulfilling both roles, use your regular leave-in, followed by a heat protectant product.

If your goal is to define curls while reducing frizz and drying time, use a diffuser to dry and set curls. Hold the blow dryer at least six inches from the hair. Focus blow dryer on individual sections of hair for no more than twenty seconds before moving on. Do this until the entire head of hair is mostly dry. It doesn't have to be completely dry. Just dry the hair enough to set curls and remove the majority of moisture.

If you want to create a blowout look, use the tension method to stretch and lengthen hair. Part hair into several sections. Twist each section and allow hair to air dry. The hair should be 70 to 90% dry *before* you begin blowdrying.

Untwist one large section. Divide that section into smaller, mini-sections. Clip the remainder of that section up and out of the way. The hair should be mostly free of tangles, since you detangled it earlier. If you encounter tangles, patiently finger detangle the section. Next, hold the mini-section near the ends, putting *slight* tension on the hair. Apply medium heat from the blow dryer to that section. Start at the roots and work your way down to the ends. Don't concentrate heat in one area for more than twenty seconds at a time. If you're afraid of damaging fragile ends, don't apply heat to the very end of the hair. Keep it covered with your hand as you apply gentle tension to the hair. Once that mini-section is dry, twist the hair into a two-strand twist. Then move on to the next mini-section. Do this until the entire section of the hair has been blown dry. Take down the next section. Part it into mini-sections. Then begin the process again. Repeat until the entire head is dry.

Remember, you are not trying to get the hair bone straight. The goal is to stretch and lengthen the hair to give it a different look. Expect to still see some of the texture. To create a style on blow-dried hair, you can leave the hair in the small two-strand twists, use twist or flex style rollers or style the hair in a bun.

At this point, you may be tempted to use a flat iron or curling iron to get the hair straighter or to achieve a curly style right away. However, remember that your child's hair has already endured the stress of a blow dryer. Using additional heating tools applies additional heat which can further stress or damage the hair. Therefore, I don't recommend using a second heat-styling tool.

If you'd like to get the look of "straightened" or stretched hair without risking damage from heat styling tools, try roller setting your child's hair with a curler that won't pull the hair (i.e. no sponge curlers). Once the hair dries completely, take down hair and separate twists or curls. The hair will be stretched. Your child can wear this style for a while. Then you can band the hair in a bun or a ponytail on top of the head to further stretch the hair. Just don't make the band so tight that it puts tension on the hairline or makes it uncomfortable for the child to sleep at night.

Another option is to skip the roller setting or twisting and just go straight to a bun or pineapple (ponytail on top of the head). However, allow the hair to air dry until it's mostly dry before securing with a ponytail maker. Use a ponytail maker that doesn't have metal parts and is gentle on the hair.

Lastly, you can try banding to lengthen the hair and give you a blow-dried look. Get a large bundle of ponytail makers that are safe for natural hair. Section air-dried hair in two or four sections. Dampen hair with a spritz of water and then add an oil or hair butter to seal in moisture. Put the first band on the hair, as you generally do when making a ponytail. Get as close to the scalp as possible. The ponytail should be tight enough to pull hair straight, but not so tight that it creates tension on the scalp or hairline. Take the next ponytail maker and band that same section of hair an inch or two down. Repeat, moving down the section until only a small section remains loose at the bottom. Put a bit of oil or hair butter on your fingers and either twist or twirl this last piece.

Do the same thing to the remaining sections of the hair. This protective style can be worn for as long as you'd like. If you are banding strictly for the straightening effect, carefully remove the hairbands the next day and separate each section with your fingers. You'll have nice, stretched hair the child can wear, as is, or you can use it as the base for other styles.

We've covered a few styling basics in this section, but in the next part of the book we'll discuss a few basic styles in more depth.

Section IV
Styling Guide

Chapter Fourteen
The Myth of the Wash and Go

With all the time and effort you've already put into pre-pooing, washing, conditioning and detangling your child's curly or kinky hair, you're probably ready for a simple, easy styling solution. To that end, a wash and go sounds like the perfect option. However, creating a healthy, beautiful, well-defined wash and go requires a little more effort than this style's carefree name suggests. Let's explore what it takes to achieve and maintain a wash and go on your child's textured hair.

Tools & Products

- Wide-tooth comb

- Rattail comb

- Spray bottle filled with water and aloe vera juice mixture

- Water-based leave-in conditioner

- Curl-defining gel

How to Achieve the Look

1. Begin with healthy, moisturized hair that has been washed and conditioned.

2. Check the directions on your curl-defining hair product. Some products recommend application to damp hair. If so, squeeze out excess water, but leave hair <u>very</u> wet. Other products require that the hair remain soaking wet in order to achieve optimal results.

3. Use the rattail comb to create smaller sections that are easier to work with. The length and thickness of your child's hair will determine the appropriate size of each section. Start from the

back and part one section. Use large butterfly clips to secure remaining hair out of the way. Use clips that won't damage hair.

4. Apply a creamy, water-based leave-in conditioner to the section. Use a wide-tooth comb to evenly distribute the product throughout. This will also remove remaining tangles.

5. Working on the same section, apply the curl-defining product using the finger shingling method. Pick up a dollop of the hair product with your fingers. Apply it to your child's hair by raking your fingers through each section. The amount of product required for each section will vary, based on the product and the texture, thickness and porosity of your child's hair. Start by following the manufacturer's suggestion. Adjust the amount used, as needed. Work the product through the hair from the roots to the ends.

6. Saturate each strand with the product. Otherwise, any hair not coated with the product will dry frizzy and fluffy, marring your finished look.

7. Smooth and stretch the hair downward, lengthening each section as you comb your fingers through the strands. Allow the curls to clump together in their natural curl pattern, creating definition. Once you've raked your fingers through a section, allow the hair to fall into place. Don't disturb it any further. Unnecessary manipulation contributes to frizz when the hair dries.

8. If a section dries out, use your water and aloe vera juice spray to rewet the section, as needed.

9. Repeat the steps above until you've completed the entire head of hair.

Let hair dry completely before disturbing it. Air drying works well, but will take several hours. Allow adequate time for the wash and go to dry before bedtime or another activity. For a quicker dry time, have your child sit under a hooded dryer.

When it's time for bed, protect your child's wash and go with a satin cap, a satin pillowcase or both. If your child has long hair, gather the hair in a high, loose ponytail toward the front of the head. This method is called pineappling. For medium length hair, create four loose ponytails.

To refresh the wash and go, take down the ponytails. Apply your favorite hair oil to your hands and reshape the hair as desired. If the hair is dry or needs a bit more moisture, spritz it with a mixture of water, leave-in conditioner and hair oil to refresh the look. If properly maintained, your child's wash and go style can last for several days.

The wash and go offers a great look with well-defined curls. However, for smaller children, wearing the hair in a wash and go all the time might not be the best option. Loose hair is more easily tangled and can be harder to manage. In the next chapter we'll review several versatile, long-lasting hair styles that protect the health of your child's hair and simplify your morning routine.

Chapter Fifteen
Low Manipulation and Protective Hairstyles

The kinks and bends of textured hair are its weakest points, making it more vulnerable to breakage. Factor in the fragile, dry nature of textured hair, and it's easy to see why frequent combing, brushing and manipulation of the hair damages kinky and curly strands. Low-manipulation hairstyles reduce how frequently strands are handled. The wash and go, discussed in the previous chapter, is a low manipulation style. Styles that don't require daily combing and manipulation preserve the health of the hair. Strong, healthy, moisturized strands aren't as prone to breakage and are therefore more likely to retain length.

Protective hairstyles take more time and effort to create. However, these long-term styles don't need to be redone often. Therefore, they require minimal handling. Low manipulation styles, like the wash and go, leave the ends of hair free. Protective styles are aptly named because their primary goal is to protect the fragile ends of the hair, which are most susceptible to breakage. Generally speaking, protective styles tend to take more time to create and are worn for longer periods of time. Still, the hair must be moisturized and properly maintained for the best health.

Let's consider some protective and low manipulation hairstyles that will reduce the stress of your morning routine. We'll discuss how to achieve and properly maintain each of these styles in a way that won't damage your child's hair.

Protective Hair Styles

Daily styling can be brutal on textured hair. The ends—the oldest, most fragile part of the hair—are most susceptible to breakage from daily styling and manipulation. Protective styles tuck ends away, preventing them from drying out. They also minimize breakage, which can make it appear as if your child's hair isn't growing. Here are a few protective styles I highly recommend for children.

Two Strand Twists

Two-strand twists are relatively easy to create. This is a good style to tackle if you're new to working with textured hair. To create the look, here's what you'll need.

Tools & Products

- Spray bottle with water and aloe vera juice

- Wide tooth comb for detangling

- Rattail comb for parting

- Moisturizing product

- Sealing product (olive oil, coconut oil, shea butter product, etc.)

- Butterfly clips

How to Achieve the Look

1. Begin with clean, detangled hair. Hair can be wet or dry. For crisper, more defined twists, install twists on wet hair and use a styling crème with hold. For a softer look, install twists on mostly dry hair slightly dampened with the recommended hair products.

2. If converting a wash and go or another style into two strand twists, you may detangle as you install the twists.

3. Slightly mist dry hair with the water and aloe vera juice mixture.

4. Using the rattail comb, section the hair into approximately six sections. Part from ear to ear. Then divide the top and bottom sections into at least three sections.

5. Begin with one section. Use butterfly clips to secure remaining hair out of the way.

6. Decide on the size of the twists. Thinner twists will create a tighter pattern. Larger twists will be puffier and have a looser pattern when the style is taken down. Part the hair according to the preferred twist size.

7. Secure remaining loose hair so it won't get incorporated inadvertently.

8. Detangle the section to be twisted with a wide tooth comb.

9. Apply moisturizing product to the section, ensuring adequate coverage. Next, apply the sealing or defining product.

10. Divide the full detangled section into two even pieces.

11. Grab each piece using the thumb and forefinger of each hand. Twist the two sections in a clockwise motion. Begin the twist as close to your child's scalp as possible to prevent frizzy roots.

12. Apply enough tension to keep the twist tight all the way to the end. (Don't worry, it will loosen up once you release it.)

13. Don't "borrow" hair between the pieces. This creates knots and tangles.

14. When you get to the end and can no longer twist, apply a dab of the sealing or holding product to your fingers and coil the end of the twist.

15. Repeat until the entire head of hair is twisted.

Tips for Wearing and Maintaining Two Strand Twists

Two strand twists can last for weeks. Before bedtime, smooth hair back and secure with a satin scarf or bonnet. Keep twists moisturized. Spritz *lightly* with water and aloe vera juice mixture or apply a moisturizer or a leave-in conditioner every few days. Follow up by sealing ends with a light oil or butter.

I don't recommend washing your child's hair while the twists are in. This can cause fine or kinky hair to become matted. Rub a light oil into the scalp to combat any dryness or itchiness.

Depending on the length of your child's hair, twists can be worn loose, swept into a chic updo or gathered into a ponytail or multiple ponytails. Headbands and hair bows also add a personal touch and variety to this style.

Individual Braids (Box Braids)

Creating individual braids, also called box braids, is only slightly more involved than creating twists. If you're not skilled at braiding, don't worry. You'll perfect your technique with practice. Practice on your own hair or on a doll to build your skill and confidence. You'll become an expert at the technique in no time.

Braids take a little longer to install, but they are more secure than two strand twists and typically last longer. Here's what you'll need to create a box braid style on your child's hair.

Tools & Products

- Spray bottle with water and aloe vera juice
- Wide tooth comb for detangling
- Rattail comb for parting
- Denman brush (optional)
- Moisturizing product (moisturizer or leave-in conditioner)
- Sealing product (olive oil, coconut oil, shea butter product, etc.)
- Butterfly clips

How to Achieve the Look

1. Like the twists, it's best to start with clean, detangled hair. Hair can be dry or slightly damp. You'll achieve a more defined braid on wet hair. (Something to consider if you want to transition this look to a braid out.) However, for more length and less shrinkage, allow the hair to dry first.

2. Part hair into four sections, then moisturize, using the LOC method discussed in Chapter Ten. Spritz the hair with the water and aloe vera juice mixture or a leave-in conditioner. Apply your preferred hair oil, followed by a crème, like whipped shea butter. Don't be too heavy-handed with the oil.

3. Next, decide how you want to style the child's hair. Create a side part, center part or diagonal part, as needed, for your chosen design.

4. Starting with that part, create a small section.

5. Secure remaining hair with a butterfly clip.

6. Part as needed, securing loose hair out of the way, until you have a small section to work with that is about the size you want a single braid to be.

7. Detangle the section one more time, making sure that entire piece is moisturized and the ends are coated with product. If you're using a Denman brush, use it to make sure knots and tangles are removed from the piece, paying special attention to the ends.

8. Separate hair into three equal sections.

9. Grab the middle section with the thumb and forefinger of your dominant hand, allowing the outside piece on that side to rest between the remaining fingers of that hand. Hold the remaining

piece between the fingers of your nondominant hand. Now you're ready to begin.

10. Using your dominant hand, move the outside piece held between the remaining fingers to the middle, making it the new middle section.

11. As you fold the piece in your nondominant hand over toward the middle, grasp the current middle section between the forefinger and thumb of the nondominant hand. (This is the tricky part, but you can do it!)

12. Keep consistent tension on the hair as you braid down. This creates a tighter, neater braid.

13. Repeat Steps 10-12 until you get to the end of the braid.

14. Try to finish each individual braid without stopping. Using the same rhythm and tension creates even braids with the same width from top to bottom.

15. If one piece gets shorter or skinnier as you're braiding, don't be tempted to "borrow" hair from another piece. This will create tangles and make it more difficult to remove the braid.

16. Once you get to the bottom and you can no longer continue the braiding process, swirl any loose hair around your finger, creating a curl.

17. Take a moment to admire your work, then part the next small section to be braided. Complete the entire section. Then take the clip from the next section and start again.

18. Keeping in mind your desired style, repeat steps until all hair is braided.

(**Note:** If you find it difficult to follow these written instructions, search YouTube for "how to braid children's hair" or a similar term. You'll find loads of videos on the process which you might find easier to follow.)

Tips for Wearing and Maintaining Box Braids

Braids can be worn for several weeks. If a braid loosens, apply a holding product or hair butter and re-braid. Before bedtime, smooth braids down and secure with a satin scarf or bonnet. Moisturize hair as often as needed with a moisturizer or a leave-in conditioner. Seal the ends with a light oil or butter.

Like twists, box braids can be worn a variety of ways to keep the style interesting. Embellishments like beads and shells can be added during the braiding process. Headbands, hair bows and head scarves allow your child to color coordinate her look and show off her personal style. For a different look, sweep braids into a ponytail or top knot. Create a bun or roll them into an elegant updo. And, of course, they look beautiful hanging loose.

Flat Twists & Cornrows

Flat twists and cornrows are worn flat against the scalp, rather than hanging freely. These styles are slightly more complicated to create, primarily because of the need to continuously add hair during the process. With two-strand twists and box braids, you begin the process with all of the hair needed to create the twist or braid. With flat twists and cornrows, you begin with only a portion of the hair that will comprise the braid or twist. You'll incorporate additional hair as you go.

This can be a little tricky to navigate at first, but don't get discouraged. With practice, this skill will become second nature. However, *__before you attempt flat twists or cornrows, learn to master two__* _strand twists and box braids_. Here's what you'll need to create these styles for your son or daughter.

Tools & Products

- Spray bottle with water and aloe vera juice
- Wide tooth comb for detangling
- Rattail comb for parting
- Denman brush (optional)
- Moisturizing product (moisturizer or leave-in conditioner)
- Sealing product (olive oil, coconut oil, shea butter product, etc.)
- Butterfly clips

How to Achieve the Look

As always, begin with clean, detangled hair. It is easier to create these styles on hair that is dry or only slightly damp.

1. Spritz hair slightly with water and aloe vera juice mixture. With a light hand, add some oil. Then finish off with your sealing product.

2. Decide which design you want to create. Flat twists and cornrows can be as simple as rows going from the forehead to the nape. However, with a little creativity, you can design an endless array of patterns that your child will be proud to wear.

3. With your design in mind, use the rattail comb to part the hair and secure all sections with butterfly clips.

4. Unclip the section you'll be working on. Create additional parts, as needed, until you have only the row of hair that will become the first flat twist or cornrow. Ideally, this should be in the center

of the head. Secure all remaining hair with a butterfly clip to avoid picking up loose hair.

For flat twists:

5. Finger part a section at the beginning of the row. Divide it into two equal pieces. Hold both pieces in your dominant hand. Hold the piece closest to the remaining hair between the thumb and forefinger of your dominant hand while holding the other between the remaining fingers of the dominant hand.

6. Twist one piece over the other two or three times for a firm foundation.

7. Now, use the index finger of your nondominant hand to finger part a small section of the loose hair closest to the twist. Add the new hair to the piece held between the thumb and forefinger of your dominant hand.

8. Now transfer the hair held between the remaining fingers of your dominant hand to the thumb and forefinger of your nondominant hand.

9. Next, switch the hair that includes the new addition to the remaining fingers of the dominant hand.

10. Grasp the hair in your nondominant hand with the thumb and forefinger of your dominant hand.

11. Repeat Steps 7-10 until all hair in the row has been incorporated into the flat twist. Once there is no more hair to add, twist the remaining hair down to the end, as you would with a two-strand twist. Using a dab of holding product, twirl any untwisted piece at the end around your fingers.

12. Go to the next section and repeat.

(**Note:** As above, you may find it easier to pick up this technique initially by watching it performed. Search YouTube for "how to flat twist natural hair.")

For cornrows:

13. Part a small section at the beginning. Divide it into _three_ even pieces.

14. Working close the scalp, apply even tension. Braid the hair a few times, as described in Steps 9-11 of the section on creating box braids.

15. Finger part a bit of the loose hair, just behind the braid. Add the new hair to the middle section, then continue braiding.

16. Add the next bit of hair to the new center section. Continue this process as you move down the row.

17. Once all of the loose hair is incorporated into the cornrow, continue braiding the remaining hair as you would with an individual braid.

18. Keep tension on the hair so that the braid is neat and pulled taut to the scalp. Be careful not to make the cornrow too tight, especially at the hairline. If the scalp lifts or the child complains of pain, the cornrow is too tight. This could lead to hair breakage and traction alopecia (hair loss caused by pulling too tightly on the hair, which causes stress to the scalp).

19. Add a bit of holding product to the fingers and twirl the end of the cornrow.

20. Move on to the next row, repeating Steps 5-11 until all of the hair has been braided in neat cornrows.

Tips for Wearing and Maintaining Flat Twists and Corn Rows

Flat twists and corn rows hold up well for several weeks. Keep them looking good by wrapping hair with a satin scarf, covering with a satin bonnet or sleeping on a satin pillowcase. Keep hair and scalp moisturized.

Both flat twists and cornrows are great protective styles. They keep ends tucked safely away and eliminate the need for manipulation of the hair. However, neither style is flexible once installed. Since the hairstyle will remain the same for as long as the child wears it, use a bit of creativity when planning the design. Try creating interesting patterns like zigzags or heart shapes. As your skill level increases, work with your child to create a fun design that he or she will enjoy throughout the life of the hairstyle.

Low Manipulation Hair Styles

Low manipulation hairstyles provide the best of both worlds. These styles reduce the need for excessive combing, brushing or finger manipulation. Yet, they are relatively easy to create and don't require your child to sit for long periods of time. With minimal maintenance, most styles can be worn for several days. In some instances, the styles can be worn even longer. Low manipulation styles have the added benefit of being versatile, allowing for different looks. That makes low manipulation styles ideal for a child who is easily bored with the same look. Here are a few low manipulation styles I recommend for children:

- Ponytails – Section hair into one or several ponytails using natural hair safe ponytail makers.

- Afro puffs – Essentially a ponytail in which the band isn't as tight, allowing the hair to look fuller. You can create one large afro puff or divide your child's hair into several afro puffs.

- Bun – Gather hair in either a high bun atop the head or into a low bun at the nape. Brush with a boar bristle brush to smooth the hair. Secure with a natural hair safe ponytail maker. Use an edge control or styling gel product like Eco Styler Olive Oil Styling Gel to smooth the hair down. Fan the gathered hair out in a circle. If the hair is long enough, you can twist and pin it into a bun. Otherwise, you can use a hair donut or bun maker to give the bun its shape by following the directions provided with the product.

- Bantu knots – Start at the front of the head on clean, detangled, mostly dry hair. Part the hair into triangle-shaped sections. Secure the hair with an elastic into a skinny ponytail at the center of each section. Re-moisturize and detangle the small ponytail. Holding it at the very end, twist the hair until you've twisted it all the way down to the scalp. Now hold the hair directly above the elastic and wind the twisted hair around that piece, tucking the ends beneath the elastic. Go to the next section and repeat. Another option is to part hair, form two-strand twists, then wind each two-strand twist into a bantu knot.

The Do's and Don'ts of Protective Styling

Protective styles are a great way to create styles that last a long time, reduce the wear and tear on hair and give you and your child a break from the styling routine. However, there a few things to keep in mind.

- Don't pull hair too tightly around the nape and edges. Undue tension on these naturally weaker areas can cause thinning.

- Don't keep the style in too long. Hair will begin to tangle.

- Don't create braids that are too small. They are more difficult to take down, resulting in overmanipulation of the hair.

- Don't choose styles that are too extravagant. This can result in breakage due to overmanipulation.

- Don't neglecting moisturizing. The hair will become dry, leading to breakage.

- Do moisturize the hair regularly.

- Do protect the hair at night with a silk or satin bonnet or a silk pillowcase.

- Do remove protective style with patience and care.

- Do dampen hair with water and conditioner while taking style down.

After all of the work you put into twisting or braiding your child's hair, you might be reluctant to take the style down. However, once loosened, braids and twists offer a whole new look. The wavy, patterned texture of a braid out or twist out will last for several days, if maintained properly. Just gather longer hair into a high ponytail near the front of the head (pineapple) and secure the hair with a silk or satin bonnet overnight. In the morning, refresh the style by spritzing the hair with moisturizer, apply a sealant and reshape.

With a wide variety of options to choose from, protective styles can be worn by everyone from very young children to adults. However, as your child gets older, she might inquire about a more permanent option for dealing with her kinky or curly hair. In the next chapter, we'll discuss some of the pros and cons of opting for a permanent relaxer to straighten the hair.

Chapter Sixteen
The Straight Truth About Relaxers

Many parents have opted to permanently straighten their daughters' hair with a chemical relaxer. Some do so because they feel that the work required to maintain natural hair is overwhelming. Some choose a relaxer because they consider the child's natural texture to be too "nappy" or otherwise inferior.

Perhaps you've mused about how much easier it would be to care for your child's hair if it were straight and glossy. However, applying a chemical straightener to achieve bone straight hair can have serious, long-term consequences.

Chemical relaxers permanently alter the structure of natural hair using an alkaline product that has a high pH level. Relaxers come in a range for formulas from "kiddie" to super strength. However, even a "kiddie" relaxer can have a pH of 9 or more. The hair shaft sustains damage, especially at higher pH levels. The hair shaft swells and the cuticles lift, making it more difficult for the strand to retain vital moisture.

In the weeks after the application of a relaxer, new hair grows in the child's natural texture. The line where coily hair meets chemically-straightened hair is particularly fragile and susceptible to breakage. It must be handled with extreme care.

Typically, in six to eight weeks the chemical relaxer must be reapplied to the new growth. The relaxer should not be reapplied to previously relaxed hair. Doing so causes further damage to chemically-weakened strands.

Lye and no-lye relaxers are the most common types available. Many consumers believe that no-lye relaxers, available in a box at your local drugstore for at-home application, are safer. However, both types of relaxers rely on similar chemicals to break down the hair bond and permanently alter it. No-lye relaxers leave calcium deposits on the hair, making it harder for strands to absorb essential moisture. Additionally, no-lye relaxers are typically applied by consumers without proper training in application of the product. This greatly increases the potential of the hair being damaged.

While typically applied by a professional, lye relaxers can also cause serious damage to the hair and scalp. The use of chemical relaxers can cause problems ranging from mild scalp irritation to chemical burns and hair loss. Long-term exposure to the chemicals in relaxers can also lead to respiratory problems.

Ultimately, the decision to relax your child's hair or not is up to you and your child. However, if your daughter expresses a sudden desire to relax her hair, try to discern the real reason behind her request. If your child is the only one in her school or classroom with kinky or curly hair, the request might be her way of desperately trying to fit in.

Rather than helping your child erase the trademark features that set her apart, lovingly reassure her that it is those very differences that make her unique and beautiful. Reference your child's hair with terms and a tone that is warm and respectful. Regularly expose your child to positive images of kinky and curly hair in all of its glory. Boost your child's confidence so she won't feel the need to straighten her hair simply to fit in.

If your daughter still wishes to straighten her hair, and you find her choice preferable, try a temporary solution first. Take your child to a natural hair care specialist who can help you find non-permanent solutions to straightening your child's hair. You can always opt for a chemical straightener when the child is older, if that is what you decide.

However, if you follow the guidelines for caring for your child's natural hair that have been outlined in this book, both you and your child should find the process of caring for her hair far less intimidating.

Chapter Seventeen
A Final Word of Encouragement

Caring for your child's natural hair can be a challenge. When one undertakes the process without any experience with kinky or curly hair, it can surely be intimidating. You undoubtedly picked up this guide because you were feeling some level of confusion or frustration about how to care for your child's hair. This book has provided insight into how to properly care for textured hair. Hopefully, that increased knowledge and understanding has also greatly increased your confidence level, too.

This book was designed to serve as both a reference and a handy how-to guide. So don't just read about the techniques outlined within the pages of this book. Be willing to dive in and try them out.

Know that your first attempt won't be perfect and neither will your second. Still, the more you put each technique into practice, the better you will become at it. Soon, you'll be both proficient and confident when it comes to caring for your child's natural hair. It is a confidence that your child will notice and appreciate, too.

There may be some areas with which you'll need more assistance. Don't be afraid to ask for help. If you run into problems beyond the scope of your knowledge, take your child to a natural hair stylist for a consultation. A natural hair care professional will be happy to answer your questions and provide recommendations tailored to your child's unique needs.

For ongoing tips on how to care for natural hair, visit MyHoneyChild.com and scroll down to join my newsletter list.

Product Recommendations

Finding the right products for your child will take some trial and error. However, these highly-recommended products are a good place to begin your child's natural hair journey. As suggested earlier, keep a log of the products used and the results achieved. Otherwise, it is easy to forget which products you've used before without success.

The products are broken down into categories.

Shampoos

- MYHoneyChild Honey Nut Scalp Cleanser
- MYHoneyChild Olive You Scalp Cleanser

Conditioners

- MYHoneyChild Honey Nutt Conditioner

Leave-in Conditioners

- MYHoneyChild O'Honey Curl Mist
- MYHoneyChild Herbal Hair Cocktail
- MYHoneyChild Aloe Vera Leave-In

Deep conditioners

- MYHoneychild Honey Hair Mask
- MYHoneyChild Olive You Deep Conditioner

Moisturizers

- MYHoneyChild Type 4 Hair Crème (For thick hair only)

Oils & Butters

- MYHoneyChild Buttery Soy Hair Creme

References

1. Audrey Davis-Sivasothy, *The Science of Black Hair* (Stafford: Saja Publishing Company, LLC, 2011)

2. Ayana D. Byrd and Lori L. Tharps, *Hair Story: Untangling the Roots of Black Hair in America* (New York: St. Martin's Griffin, 2014)

3. Tracey Owens Patton. "Hey Girl, Am I More than My Hair?: African American Women and Their Struggles with Beauty, Body Image, and Hair." NWSA Journal 18, no. 2 (Summer 2006): 24-51.

4. Cheryl Thompson, *Black Women and Identity: What's Hair Got to Do With It?* (Ann Arbor, MI: MPublishing, University of Michigan Library, Fall 2008-2009) vol. 22, no. 1.

66512949R00061

Made in the USA
Columbia, SC
17 July 2019